MW00465942

Proclaiming Shalom

Lectionary Introductions
to Foster
the Catholic and Jewish Relationship

Philip A. Cunningham

Proclaiming Shalom

Lectionary Introductions
to Foster
the Catholic and Jewish
Relationship

A PUEBLO BOOK

The Liturgical Press   Collegeville, Minnesota

A Pueblo Book published by The Liturgical Press

Design by Frank Kacmarcik

© 1995 by The Order of St. Benedict, Inc., Collegeville, Minnesota. All rights reserved. No part of this book may be reproduced in any form or by any means, electronic or mechanical, including photocopying, recording, taping, or any retrieval system, without the written permission of The Liturgical Press, Collegeville, Minnesota 56321. Printed in the United States of America.

Library of Congress Cataloging-in-Publication Data

Cunningham, Philip A.
    Proclaiming shalom : lectionary introductions to foster the
Catholic and Jewish relationship / Philip A. Cunningham ; foreword
by Eugene J. Fisher and Leon Klenicki.
        p.   cm.
    "A Pueblo book."
    Includes bibliographical reference.
    ISBN 0-8146-6142-4
    1. Lectionaries.   2. Mass commentators.   3. Christianity and
antisemitism.   4. Catholic Church—Relations—Judaism.   5. Judaism—
Relations—Catholic Church.   6. Catholic Church—Liturgy.
7. Catholic Church—Doctrines.   I. Title.
BX2003.C86   1995
264'.02034—dc20   95-10574
                                                                    CIP

Dedicated to the Catholic Community of
SAINT MARK the EVANGELIST PARISH
Londonderry, New Hampshire

Contents

Foreword by Eugene J. Fisher and Leon Klenicki   ix

Introduction   1

1. Advent   23

2. Christmas   31

3. Lent   37

4. Easter   51

5. Ordinary Time   67

6. Feasts   124

7. Recommended Resources   134

Foreword

Proclaiming Shalom fills a real need for Catholic parishes and other Christian congregations that use the common lectionary. It provides in a single volume very brief introductory remarks for the Sunday biblical portions for all three cycles. Reflecting the best of contemporary Jewish and Christian biblical scholarship, the introductions are at the same time eminently practical and, as is said, "user-friendly." They can be read from the pulpit before the proclamation of the Scriptural texts, or inserted in the Sunday bulletin—or both.

They were developed by the author over a three-year period directly for use in his home parish, the Catholic community of (appropriately enough) St. Mark the Evangelist, and first used (and refined) there. So they have been tested in practice.

The remarks have a two-fold aim. First, they are meant to meet the need for general explanatory introductions to biblical passages just as do any such "pre-reading" introductions in missalettes or other lectionary aids. They are designed for normal use in parishes and do not require any special situations or instructions to the congregation. They stand on their own as the work of a fine author whose background lies in Catholic education and Sacred Scripture.

But within this overall goal, the introductions contained here also reflect, to use the words of the 1974 Guidelines of the Holy See, an "overriding preoccupation" to present the lectionary readings with sensitivity to the portrait they may convey of Jews and Judaism. The author's Introduction explains quite well why this is so and why the Catholic Church has mandated the development of just the kind of material for use in the liturgy as is embodied so well in *Proclaiming Shalom.* Suffice it to say here that, insofar as we know, the reader now holds in his or her hands the very first full-scale attempt to implement the mandate of the Holy See's 1974 Guidelines to "apply [the fruits of Catholic-Jewish dialogue] to introductions to biblical readings." Parishes that use this volume will have the chance to make a bit of history for the Church.

We would also point out that Dr. Cunningham's introductions are designed not only to correct previous misunderstandings of Jews and Judaism that Christians might have fallen into based on superficial readings of the biblical texts, as his Introduction shows, but they also bring out, time after time, exciting new aspects of the texts we have listened to year after year by bringing to bear on them some of the great spiritual insights of Jewish tradition. This book will not only help us avoid certain errors of the past but will be in many ways a "wake-up call" to our congregations to look at familiar texts from what is for Christians a fresh new vantage point. This dual dynamic of correction and enrichment provides *Proclaiming Shalom* with a dynamism and sense of discovery that can help to enliven Sunday worship.

We trust your parish will enjoy these introductions as much as the author's parish has over the past three years. We, along with the author, would be most interested in receiving any comments you might have based on your experience with them.

Eugene J. Fischer
Leon Klenicki
Shavuoth/Pentecost, 1995

Introduction

A. General Purposes

Proclaiming Shalom is a collection of introductory remarks to be made before the proclamation of the Scripture readings at Sunday worship. It frames the lectionary excerpts in ways that promote both the Catholic appreciation of the Hebrew tradition and the relationship between modern Jews and Christians.

It might well be asked why there is a need for such comments. There are basically two answers: (1) Spiritual maturity in the Christian faith requires an accurate understanding of Judaism, both past and present, and (2) certain lectionary selections can promote anti-Jewish attitudes if they are heard outside of their historical contexts.

The first point has been made in several Catholic documents issued since the ground-breaking 1965 Second Vatican Council declaration *Nostra Aetate*. For example, a 1974 Vatican statement noted that ". . . the spiritual bonds and historical links binding the Church to Judaism . . . render obligatory a better mutual understanding and renewed mutual esteem. . . . Christians must therefore strive to acquire a better knowledge of the basic components of the religious tradition of Judaism; they must strive to learn by what essential traits the Jews define themselves in the light of their own religious experience."[1]

More recently, Pope John Paul II, during a visit to a synagogue in Rome, stressed the closeness of the two traditions: "The Church of Christ discovers her 'bond' with Judaism by 'searching into her own mystery' (cf. *Nostra Aetate*). The Jewish religion is not 'extrinsic' to us, but in a certain way is 'intrinsic' to our own religion. With Judaism therefore we have a relationship which we do not have with any other religion. You [Jews] are our dearly beloved brothers and, in a certain way, it could be said that you are our elder brothers."[2]

Because of these close links between Judaism and Christianity, it would seem that a distorted image of one will inevitably produce warped ideas about the other.[3] Therefore, in order for Christians to understand their own faith properly they must possess a truthful grasp of Judaism.

Since the Sunday liturgy provides the sole occasion for the ongoing religious education of most adult Catholics, it is all the more important that "With respect to liturgical readings, care will be taken to see that homilies based on them will not distort their meaning, especially when it is a question of passages which seem to show the Jewish people as such in an unfavorable light. Efforts will be made so to instruct the Christian people that they will understand the true interpretation of all the texts and their meaning for the contemporary believer. . . . [These] remarks also apply to introductions to biblical readings, to the Prayer of the Faithful, and to commentaries printed in missals. . . ."[4]

As will be seen below, biblical passages excerpted in the lectionary impact on Christian attitudes regarding Judaism in several ways: (1) the revelatory value of the Hebrew Bible, (2) the issue of prediction and fulfillment, (3) the character of Judaism, (4) the depiction of the Pharisees, (5) the death of Jesus, and (6) the permanence of God's covenant with the Jewish people. Without some advance preparation, there is a real danger that the lectionary will produce negative, or at best inaccurate, ideas about Jews and Judaism in each of these areas.

The second reason for these introductions was brought out very forcefully in a recent analysis of the presentation of Jews and Judaism in Roman Catholic religion textbooks. This study found that the most negative statements were made in reference to certain biblical themes. These included the relationship of Jesus to Jewish contemporaries; the Pharisees; and the crucifixion. In many cases, the negativity of these subjects was caused by the uncritical citation of biblical texts that had originated in argumentative circumstances.[5]

As members of one Jewish renewal movement among many, the first proclaimers of Jesus as the Raised Lord engaged in disputation with other Jewish groups using the somewhat fiery rhetorical standards of the first-century world.[6] Some of this argumentative speech was eventually preserved in the canon of the New Testament. Once so enshrined, however, these polemics took on a life of their own, acquiring new meanings when later read in different social contexts. For instance, complaints originally leveled by some Jews against other Jews eventually came to be read by later Gentiles as factual statements about the defects of Jews universally. Without reading these sorts of passages in their own historical contexts, they assume a virulent anti-Jewish tone and promote animosity between Jews and Christians today.[7]

This was the principal difficulty with the religion textbooks mentioned earlier which scored negatively in terms of their portrayal of Jews and Judaism. By failing to reckon critically with the originating contexts of certain polemical passages, anti-Jewish caricatures were propagated. Since some of these same polemical passages are selections in the three-year lectionary cycle, the Sunday readings have the potential to foster false stereotypes of Judaism and hostility to modern Jews, at least when such readings are simply proclaimed without explanation or comment.

For example, there is a tendency in all the Gospels to shift responsibility for Jesus' death away from Pontius Pilate and onto Jews.[8] This happened for several reasons. When the Gospels were composed, in the last third of the first century, the Church was gradually becoming less and less a Jewish renewal group and more and more a Gentile movement. Obtaining legal status in the Roman Empire as a legitimate religion was a priority for the emerging Christian community. This aim would not be helped by emphasizing the embarrassing fact that the Church's founder had been executed as a pretender-king by the orders of a Roman prefect. The evangelists dealt with this by having Pilate declare Jesus' innocence three times (Luke 23:4, 14, 22), by having Jews accept responsibility for the death sentence (Matt 27:25), or by having a reluctant and indecisive Pilate succumb to Jewish threats (John 19:12-16). These tactics had the additional benefits of denouncing Jewish rivals of the early Church and of distancing the Church from those Jews who had unsuccessfully rebelled against Rome in their 66–70 war.

The influence of this first-century social dynamic on an unaware twentieth-century audience is very important in the post–*Nostra Aetate* Church. It could be argued that, lacking a basic familiarity with the historical contexts of the Gospel accounts, modern congregations experience a refresher course in anti-Jewish sentiment each year during Holy Week. Therefore, "homilists and catechists should seek to provide a proper context for the proclamation of the passion narratives."[9] One way this can be done is through lectionary introductions.

In short, the lectionary introductions in this book seek to advance the Catholic and Jewish relationship so that an accurate knowledge of the Christian faith is engendered and the hazards of promoting anti-Judaism are reduced. The book's title, *Proclaiming Shalom*, conveys this dual purpose. The Hebrew word *shalom* denotes, among other things, the peace that stems from wholeness and right relationship. By proclaiming shalom, the Church confirms its rootedness in Judaism, enhances its friendship with the contemporary Jewish people and tradition, and becomes more whole, more authentically Christian, as a result.

B. The Sunday Lectionary and Biblical Interpretation

Composing introductions to the liturgical Scripture readings is a daunting task. It cannot be forgotten that such comments are at the service of the sacred texts and the faithful.[10] Members of the congregation ought to be left as free as possible to encounter and seek meaning in the readings according to their individual and unique spiritualities and life experiences. A narrowing of the polyvalent richness of the Scriptures into a monolithic flatness should be avoided as much as possible.

On the other hand, some restraints have already been put onto the biblical passages by the very act of excerpting them and juxtaposing them with other scriptural extracts. Those who in the aftermath of Vatican II were responsible for formulating the lectionary cycle have made interpretative decisions about the texts. Even within a particular biblical passage, certain verses were included, omitted, or combined in order to speak to overarching themes determined by the liturgical season or feast. It may be that in some cases these selections were not sensitive to the dynamics of the Jewish and Christian relationship as discussed above. After all, the lectionary was devised in the late 1960s, whereas many of the principles of *Nostra Aetate* were not fully developed and advanced until after that time.

Therefore, lectionary introductions in the service of promoting Christian and Jewish amity must respect the sacred character of the biblical texts and help elicit their meanings in a way that does not overwhelm them with excessive commentary. At the same time, however, such introductions have an obligation to nuance those texts whose selection or juxtaposition can produce consequences that were not realized by the architects of the lectionary and which are now disavowed in the Catholic tradition.

This leads to the general topic of biblical interpretation. There are many Sundays when some or all of the readings do not contain explicit references to sensitive issues in terms of Jews and Christians. How do these lectionary introductions function in such instances?

This collection has "an overriding preoccupation to bring out explicitly the meaning of a text, while taking scriptural studies into account."[11] For Catholics, the meaning of a biblical text is first to be sought in the intentions of the sacred authors.[12] These intentions are pursued by situating the biblical text as much as possible in its social and historical context and in terms of its relationships with other biblical and relevant extrabiblical materials.[13]

Therefore, these introductions will often proceed by briefly providing some historical or literary background so that the congregation may hear the readings in an appropriate context. If a particular biblical book is to be consecutively presented for several weeks, a short explanation of its origins and setting may be offered. In practice, the need for such historical data arises most frequently in the case of the first and second readings, which offer portions of a wider variety of biblical books than does the Gospel reading. With biblical authors whose writings are frequently excerpted, especially the four evangelists, the introductions may point to an individual stylistic trait or characteristic concern (e.g., the Fourth Gospel's regular use of legal vocabulary). In this way the congregation can get to know and understand the author and his words better. At other times, the readings might suggest a reference to rabbinic or other Jewish traditions of interpretation. In the interests of promoting an awareness of the ongoing spiritual richness of Jewish thought, some introductions will offer comments in this regard.[14] Finally, with biblical selections requiring little historical background for comprehension, some questions about the implications of the reading for modern believers may be posed by regarding the congregation as dynamically equivalent to those addressed in or by the text.

The Hebrew Bible/Old Testament

The lectionary's practice of almost always presenting a passage from the Hebrew Scriptures as the first reading raises a number of complex questions in terms of biblical interpretation, liturgical setting, and attitudes toward Judaism. Most often, the first reading was selected in order to correspond with the Gospel Reading. Occasionally, this happens because the Old Testament passage is read christologically, or in reference to Jesus, and as such may transcend the intentions of the Hebrew authors in their original contexts. This is especially the case when a pattern of prediction/fulfillment is applied to the Old Testament and Gospel readings.

The practice of christologically interpreting the Hebrew Bible dates from the earliest gatherings of the first church communities. Fairly soon after experiencing the resurrection of Jesus, his followers turned to Israel's Scriptures in order to understand what had happened. Those ancient sacred texts were reinterpreted in the light of Jesus' crucifixion and resurrection.[15] As a related development, and from fairly soon after the Resurrection, the Church in its worship began to pray to the risen Jesus and to speak of him in terms that had previously been reserved for God. Probably this custom was one significant, if not the major, difference between Jews "in Christ" and other Jews.[16] It is very likely that it was in such post–resurrectional liturgical settings that Jesus' followers first began confessing his divinity.[17]

This ancient Christian custom of reading the Old Testament christologically has led one modern commentator to insist that ". . . the interpretation of the OT found in the NT (and reflected in our present lectionary) originated, at least in part, in the liturgy and played a substantial part in the creation of the NT. This interpretation is bonded into the liturgy from the beginning and could not be eliminated without doing violence to it and changing its very nature."[18]

On the other hand, there are social, educational, and pastoral issues to take into account.[19] While the need for christological readings of the Hebrew Scriptures was an inarguable feature of the life of the early Church, it was also a time of rivalry and dispute between the Jewish followers of Jesus (later augmented by Gentile believers) and other

Jewish groups. The proper interpretative approach to the Torah and the Prophets was one issue under debate and tended to mark out the borders among the various groups.[20] In accord with the customs of the time, sometimes this boundary delineation was accompanied by invective and polemic (e.g., Matt 23; Acts 6:8–7:55, especially 7:51-53). A christological reading of the Hebrew Bible, then, was also related to the early Church's efforts to define the boundaries between itself and other Jews.

The use of christological approaches to the Hebrew Bible affected attitudes toward Jews and Judaism. This was especially the case in the patristic period, when Christian beliefs were formulaically defined and credally confessed.[21]

Biblical interpretation, therefore, produces social effects. I would argue that the extent to which an exclusively christological use of the Old Testament delegitimizes the original meaning in the author's context or the alternative readings of past and present Jews, to that extent a christological approach is marking boundaries in a way that is destructive of interreligious amity, and indeed can result in intergroup hostility.

Although fundamental to the beginnings of Christian worship, it does not follow that first-century christological readings of the Hebrew Bible must be the only perspectives employed in a twentieth-century Church that has become aware of the historical dangers of heedlessly recycling ancient intergroup polemic. A more sophisticated christological approach for liturgical use, one that confesses Christian belief while simultaneously respecting the text on its own terms, seems to be required.

In this regard, recent Catholic ecclesial documents have called attention to nonchristological readings of the Hebrew Scriptures. The 1974 Vatican "Guidelines" declared, "that an effort will be made to acquire a better understanding of whatever in the Old Testament retains its own perpetual value (cf. *Dei Verbum* 14–15), since that has not been canceled by the later interpretation of the New Testament."[22]

A decade later, the Vatican "Notes" observed that typological readings of the Old Testament, approaches that relate Israelite figures/events to Christ, "manifest the unfathomable riches of the Old Testament, its inexhaustible content and the mystery of which it is full, and should not lead us to forget that it retains its own value as revelation that the New Testament often does no more than resume (cf. Mark 12:29-31)."[23]

Most recently, the United States Bishops' Committee on the Liturgy advised Catholic preachers to:

"Consistently affirm the value of the whole Bible. While 'among all the Scriptures, even those of the New Testament, the Gospels have a special preeminence' (*Dei Verbum*, 18), the Hebrew Scriptures are the word of God and have validity and dignity in and of themselves (ibid., 15). Keep in view the intentions of the biblical authors (ibid., 19).

"Communicate a reverence for the Hebrew Scriptures and avoid approaches that reduce them to a propadeutic or background for the New Testament. It is God who speaks, communicating himself through divine revelation (*Dei Verbum*, 6)."[24]

Based on such guidelines, these lectionary introductions will first comment upon the historical contexts and authorial intentions of readings from the Hebrew Scriptures. In instances where christological implications were obviously intended by the lectionary compilers, these will be noted only after the historical discussion. In such cases a phrase similar to, "This passage reminds Christians of Jesus, who also . . . " will be employed. A formulation of this type preserves the integrity of the Hebrew Bible on its own terms while also recognizing the resonances the text has with later christological interpretations.

Terminologically, these introductions will consistently make reference to "the Hebrew Bible or the Hebrew Scriptures," rather than to the more traditional "Old Testament." This is not because the term "Old Testament" *must* demean Judaism.[25] However, given the lectionary's practice of choosing Hebrew Bible passages for coherence with the Gospel reading, the use of alternative vocabulary will highlight the integral revelatory value of the Hebrew Scriptures. The "Hebrew" in the phraseology employed herein refers not to the Hebrew language in which most of the texts are written, but to the Hebraic or Israelite tradition from which those sacred writings come.[26]

C. The Issue of Prediction/Fulfillment

Debates about the relationship between the Testaments come to a precise focus with the topic of prediction and fulfillment. On a number of Sundays, particularly those during Advent, excerpts from the Prophets are juxtaposed with Gospel selections in such a way that it appears that an ancient Hebrew prophet predicted details about the life or death of Jesus.

As mentioned above, this utilization of the Hebrew Scriptures has roots in Second Temple Judaism and in the New Testament itself. For example, prophetic texts that had never before been considered messianic became so to Christians who reinterpreted them in the light of the resurrection.[27]

There are two points to be made concerning how the introductions in this book will deal with such passages. As stated above, the first step will be to situate the prophetic text in its own historical setting. The prophets will primarily be understood as the consciences of the covenant in their own eras whose words, to be sure, had implications for the future.

One such future meaning, namely the connection of the first reading with the Gospel, will then be described in terms of its "resonances" with the Christ event. In other words, the prophetic declaration will be understood as an expression of a pattern of relationship between God and God's people that recurs and is seen by Christians most profoundly in the life of Jesus. For example, the suffering servant songs of Isaiah of the Exile can be described as an inspired insight that the suffering of the righteous can be hallowed by God and thereby produce unexpected blessings. This principle is seen by Christians to be most powerfully manifested in the crucifixion of Jesus. This approach, which avoids a simplistic and exegetically inaccurate prediction/fulfillment motif, highlights the prophet's revelatory value and honors the Christian application of the prophet's words to Jesus. At the same time, it keeps the prophetic declaration open-ended; its significance is not exhausted in Christ but can continue to impart meaning to ongoing human experience. Isaiah's message can continue to provide solace to those who suffer today.

Secondly, if the above remarks nuance what is meant by "prediction," recent ecclesial documents have reconfigured the meaning of "fulfillment." The 1974 Vatican Guidelines introduced an eschatological element into the discussion of prediction/fulfillment by declaring that, "We [Christians] believe that [Torah] promises were fulfilled with the first coming of Christ. But it is nonetheless true that we still await their perfect fulfillment in His glorious return at the end of time."[28]

The 1985 Vatican "Notes" furthered this idea in its treatment of typology. Typology is the use of Hebrew Scriptures as "types" that foreshadow their ultimate expression in the person of the "antitype," namely, Christ.[29] The "Notes" explain:

"Typology further signifies reaching toward an accomplishment of the divine plan, when 'God will be all in all' (1 Cor 15:28). This holds true also for the Church which, realized already in Christ, yet awaits its definitive perfection as the body of Christ. The fact that the body of Christ is still tending toward its full stature (cf. Eph 4:12-19) takes nothing from the value of being a Christian. So also the calling of the patriarchs and the Exodus from Egypt do not lose their importance and value in God's design from being at the same time intermediate stages (cf. e.g., *Nostra Aetate*, 4)."[30]

In this passage, the "Notes" categorize the patriarchs, the Exodus experience, *and* the Body of Christ as types of the great eschatological antitype of the future—the establishment in its fullness of the reign of God. This puts both the Hebrew Bible and the New Testament in typological relationship to the ultimate future. The Hebrew Bible is not simply a type of the New Testament, the prophets are not just types of Christ; all typify creation's uttermost destiny when the reign of God is realized.

This vantage point permitted the "Notes" to stress another aspect of the relationship of the Testaments:

"Furthermore, in underlining the eschatological dimension of Christianity we shall reach a greater awareness that the people of God of the Old and New Testaments are tending toward a like end in the future: the coming or the return of the Messiah—even if they start from two different points of view. It is more clearly understood that the person of the Messiah is not only a point of division for the people of God but also a point of convergence. . . . Attentive to the same God who has spoken, hanging on the same word, we have to witness to one same memory and one common hope in [the One] who is the master of history. We must also accept our responsibility to prepare the world for the coming of the Messiah by working together for social justice, respect for the rights of persons and nations and for social and international reconciliation. To this we are driven, Jews and Christians, by the command to love our neighbor, by a common hope for the kingdom of God, and by the great heritage of the prophets. Transmitted soon enough by catechesis, such a conception would teach young Christians in a practical way to cooperate with Jews, going beyond simple dialogue."[31]

Clearly, by emphasizing that fulfillment has yet to occur fully, the common mission of both Jews and Christians is accentuated. This provides a useful approach to the Advent lectionary readings, as was made clear by the United States Bishops' Committee on the Liturgy. In their 1988 guidelines, one finds the most detailed discussion of the question of prophecy/fulfillment to appear in any ecclesial document to date:

"The [Advent] lectionary readings from the prophets are selected to bring out the ancient Christian theme that Jesus is the 'fulfillment' of the biblical message of hope and promise, the inauguration of the 'days to come'. . . . This truth needs to be framed very carefully. Christians believe that Jesus is the promised Messiah who has come, but also know that his messianic kingdom is not yet fully realized. The ancient messianic prophecies are not merely temporal predictions but profound expressions of eschatological hope. Since this dimension can be misunderstood or even missed altogether, the homilist needs to raise clearly the hope found in the prophets and heightened in the proclamation of Christ. This hope includes trust in what is promised but not yet seen. While the biblical prophecies of an age of universal *shalom* are 'fulfilled' (i.e., irreversibly inaugurated) in Christ's coming, that fulfillment is not yet completely worked out in each person's life or perfected in the world at large. It is the mission of the Church, as also that of the Jewish people, to proclaim and to work to prepare the world for the full flowering of God's Reign, which is, but is 'not yet.'"[32]

The redefinition of "fulfillment" is very notable. Usually understood as the achievement of some goal that had earlier been set, the Committee's formulation presents "fulfillment" as "irreversibly inaugurating," a process that will not be finally attained until the coming of the Raised One in glory. The consequent possibilities for a positive appraisal of the ongoing Jewish tradition are obvious. Both Jews and Christians await the completion of God's reign. Both can assist and support one another in fostering that event.

Thus, these lectionary introductions will treat prediction/fulfillment passages by: (1) providing the historical context of the prophetic text, (2) noting the resonances of prophetic insights with the life and death of Jesus, and (3) pointing to the ultimate goal of all things in the eschatological future. This latter, eschatological viewpoint is especially appropriate during the Advent season.[33]

D. First-century Judaism and the Pharisees

Another difficulty regarding Christian attitudes toward Judaism emerges from the New Testament itself. Certain Pauline and Gospel passages can contribute to the false idea that first-century Judaism was a legalistic and moribund religion that Jesus came to displace. The nature of opposition to Jesus from some of his first-century Jewish contemporaries can also be easily misunderstood.

For instance, the repeated usage of the term "the Jews" in the Gospel of John suggests that all Jews were adversaries of Jesus. Lectionary excerpts from John, without some explanation, can foster such a view.[34] A parallel dynamic occurs with certain lectionary excerpts from the Acts of the Apostles during the Easter season.[35]

Similarly, the scribes and Pharisees almost always function in the readings as petty faultfinders, likely reinforcing a legalistic caricature of first-century Judaism.[36] It is unfortunate that few positive New Testament references to the Pharisees were selected for lectionary use. Such notable passages as Luke 13:31, in which some Pharisees warn Jesus about Herod Antipas, or Acts 5:33-39, where the Pharisee Gamaliel intervenes on behalf of the apostles, are not heard by Sunday worshipers.

Any caricaturing of Judaism in Catholic worship is to be avoided. As the United States bishops have urged, "An explicit rejection [should be made] of the historically inaccurate notion that Judaism of that time, especially Pharisaism, was a decadent formalism and hypocrisy, well exemplified by Jesus' enemies."[37]

Such a distorted picture of Judaism will be discouraged in these lectionary introductions in several ways. First, the rich diversity of first-century Jewish thought will be noted when appropriate.[38] There were many issues being wrestled with and argued about among the many varieties of Jews of the time. Jesus was a fully Jewish participant in this exchange, sometimes agreeing, sometimes disagreeing with his conversation partners. To make this social dynamic clear for a particular Gospel reading, an introduction might identify an opponent of Jesus as typical of one strain of Jewish thought, with Jesus seemingly advocating another Jewish outlook. This principle was articulated by the United States Bishops' Committee on the Liturgy:

"Jesus was perhaps closer to the Pharisees in his religious vision than to any other group of his time. . . . Many scholars are of the view that Jesus was not so much arguing against 'the Pharisees' as a group, as he was condemning the excesses of some Pharisees, excesses of a sort that can be found among some Christians as well. In some cases, Jesus appears to have been participating in internal Pharisaic debates on various points of God's law. . . . Jesus' interpretation of biblical law is similar to that found in some of the prophets and ultimately adopted by rabbinic tradition as can be seen in the *Talmud*."[39]

Second, similarities between Jesus and Jewish contemporaries will be highlighted as the reading permits. This is especially true concerning the Pharisees with whom Jesus apparently had much in common: "Jesus shares, with the majority of Palestinian Jews of that time, some pharisaic doctrines: the resurrection of the body; forms of piety, like alms-giving, prayer, fasting and the liturgical practice of addressing God as Father; the priority of the commandment to love God and our neighbor . . . . [Jesus also] used methods of reading and interpreting Scripture and of teaching his disciples which were common to the Pharisees of their time."[40]

Third, when pertinent, the fact that "some references hostile or less than favorable to the Jews have their historical contexts in conflicts between the nascent Church and the Jewish community"[41] will be explained. In other words, some of the Gospel writers were engaged in local disputes with neighboring synagogues decades after the death and resurrection of Jesus. Some of their arguments appear in the Gospels, anachronistically situated in the ministry of Jesus. A vivid example of this is John 9:22 in which the parents of a man born blind fear being expelled from the synagogue by "the Jews" for confessing Jesus as the Messiah (see also 12:42 and 16:2). This scene could not arise until the last decade of the first century, when the Church was becoming a separate religious entity distinct from Judaism. By reflecting their present reality in their depictions of Jesus' ministry, the evangelists have melded different time periods.[42] Ignorance of this dynamic can cause modern congregations to assume that Jesus and his contemporaries were as divided from one another as the Church and Synagogue later became.

These three approaches will provide a more balanced understanding of Jesus within his Jewish context. While it is not possible to treat every lectionary allusion to this topic by means of introductions, passages in which first-century Judaism figure prominently will be addressed.

E. The Crucifixion

Historically, the charge of universal Jewish responsibility for the execution of Jesus has produced a long tradition of violence by Christians against Jews. The passion narratives and certain passages in the Acts of the Apostles can suggest a biblical basis for such an indictment to those who are unaware of Catholic biblical principles. As mentioned above, there were a number of factors that encouraged the Gospel writers to de-emphasize the Roman role in the crucifixion and to overstate Jewish involvement. This dynamic gives the passion narratives a latent inflammatory character, which over the centuries has incited Christian hostility toward innocent Jewish neighbors.

On this subject, the words of *Nostra Aetate* are clear:

"True, authorities of the Jews and those who followed their lead pressed for the death of Christ; still what happened in His passion cannot be blamed upon all the Jews then living, without distinction, nor upon the Jews of today. Although the Church is the new people of God, the Jews should not be presented as repudiated or cursed by God, as if such views followed from the holy scriptures. All should take pains, then, lest in catechetical instruction and in the preaching of God's word they teach anything out of harmony with the truth of the Gospel and the Spirit of Christ.

"The Church repudiates all persecutions against anyone. Moreover, mindful of her common patrimony with the Jews, . . . she deplores the hatreds, persecutions, and displays of anti-Semitism directed against the Jews at any time and from any source.

"Besides, as the Church has always held and continues to hold, Christ in His boundless love freely underwent His passion and death because of the sins of all people, so that all might attain salvation."[43]

In addition to rejecting any effort to impute a collective guilt for the crucifixion to Jews, the Council fathers also established an axiom of Catholic biblical interpretation: any reading of the New Testament which concludes that Jews are rejected or accursed by God is invalid.[44]

These lectionary introductions will address this issue in a number of ways. First, when appropriate, certain historical facts will be noted. These include that crucifixion was a Roman form of execution; that Jesus was apparently viewed by the Romans as a potential threat to imperial rule (N.B. the charge nailed on Jesus' cross); that the high priest was appointed by Pontius Pilate and retained his authority at Pilate's pleasure; that the Pharisees as a group played no role in Jesus' death; and that Jesus was sufficiently popular with the Jewish population to appear as a menace to Roman peace who needed to be taken into custody secretly. Such data highlights Roman responsibility for the crucifixion and clarifies Jewish involvement as being, in all probability, largely limited to those leaders who collaborated with the Romans to keep the peace.

Second, the tendency of the evangelists to minimize the Roman role will be noted and explained. The effects of late first-century synagogue and church dispute are also important in this regard.

Third, the traditional theological insight that Jesus died because of universal human sin will be stressed. By meditating on the crucifixion, Christians should be moved to realize their own sinfulness and need of repentance. Specifically, an awareness of the violence that has been generated over the ages by Christian abuse of the passion narratives "should lead to a deep sense of the need for reconciliation with the Jewish community today."[45]

F. The Jewish Relationship with God

The quotation from *Nostra Aetate* (footnote no. 43) touches on a final topic of importance to the Jewish and Christian relationship. This is the implication that if Jews are not rejected by God, then their covenantal bonding with God must remain in effect. Although such an idea is contrary to conventional Christian teaching over the centuries, it has been explicitly asserted several times by Pope John Paul II. He has described Jews as "the people of God of the Old Covenant, never revoked by God,"[46] as "the present-day people of the covenant concluded with Moses,"[47] and as partners in "a covenant of eternal love which was never revoked."[48] Because of this enduring bond, the Pope understands that the heritage of Judaism is above all "a living heritage, which must be understood and preserved in its depth and richness by us Catholic Christians."[49]

Although the lectionary readings rarely provide the opportunity to state this conviction, it undergirds many of the introductory references to modern Jewish practice and to various elements of the Jewish tradition. By so depicting Judaism as a vital and important religious heritage from which Catholics can benefit, the ongoing covenantal character of the Jewish community is implicitly conveyed.[50]

G. Conclusion

Hopefully the lectionary introductions in this volume will help to enable Christian worship to celebrate the Jewish tradition that has so definitively shaped our Catholic spirituality. But there are also other liturgical tasks that need attention. For example, many of the classic hymns that Christians sing at Eucharist can promote negative attitudes toward Judaism. The ancient hymn *O Come O Come Emmanuel* is possibly the quintessential Advent song. Its evocative melody instantly establishes the Advent mood. Yet, its first verse is troublesome to those sensitive to Jewish-Christian relations:

"O Come O Come Emmanuel,
And ransom captive Israel
That mourns in lonely exile here,
Until the Son of God appear."

These words do not elicit a positive feeling toward first-century Judaism. Instead, it reinforces the conventional caricature of Judaism as moribund and lifeless.

Perhaps even more illustrative of the need for hymnal reform is the *Pange, Lingua* of Thomas Aquinas, rendered into English as *Praise We Christ's Immortal Body.* This is also an ancient melody and is frequently sung on Holy Thursday or Corpus Christi. Unfortunately, two of its verses explicitly assert that the Jewish covenantal relationship with God has terminated:

"On the eve of that last supper
Breaking bread with chosen friends
He obeys the Law's directions
Even as the Old Law ends
Now he hands the twelve a new Bread
And to them himself extends

"Humbly let us voice our homage
For so great a sacrament
Let all former rites surrender
To the Lord's New Testament
What our senses fail to fathom
Let us grasp through faith's consent"

These examples point up the need for new lyrics and hymns that reflect the reform of the modern Church's attitudes toward Jews and Judaism. Earlier expressions of the Church's hostility to Judaism should not be seasonally reprised to the detriment of the rapprochement initiated by *Nostra Aetate.* Hopefully, talented musicians and liturgists will turn their attention to this matter in the near future.

Finally, it might be observed that the introductions presented in this volume are not the only ways of presenting the lectionary readings in a manner that affirms the Catholic and Jewish relationship. Even in their excerpted state, the Hebrew Scripture and New Testament readings are so rich in meaning that they could be introduced in a variety of ways.

It is my hope that this book will provide both useful introductory remarks and guidance for formulating similar comments in the future. The "Recommended Resources" at the end of the book offer further aids in shaping additional preparatory notes.

I would like to dedicate this collection to the Catholic community of St. Mark the Evangelist parish in Londonderry, New Hampshire. It was with the encouragement of the pastor, Rev. Thomas J. Bresnahan, and the pastoral associate, Mr. Lee Abbott, that these introductions were composed and implemented over the past three years of the lectionary cycle. I would also like to express my gratitude to Dr. Eugene J. Fisher and Rabbi Leon Klenicki for their support of this project.[51]

Notes

1. Vatican Commission for Religious Relations with the Jews, "Guidelines and Suggestions on Implementing the Conciliar Declaration *Nostra Aetate*, 4," Preamble, in Eugene J. Fisher and Leon Klenicki, eds., *In Our Time: The Flowering of Jewish-Catholic Dialogue* (Mahwah, N.J.: Paulist Press/Stimulus Books, 1990) 29–37.

2. John Paul II, "To the Jewish Community in Rome," (April 13, 1986) in Eugene J. Fisher and Leon Klenicki, eds., *Pope John Paul II on Jews and Judaism, 1979–1986* (Washington: USCC, 1987) 79–85.

3. Note the comment that "false or demeaning portraits of a repudiated Israel may undermine Christianity as well. How can one confidently affirm the truth of God's covenant with all humanity and creation in Christ (see Rom 8:21) without at the same time affirming God's faithfulness to the Covenant with Israel that also lies at the heart of the biblical testimony?" in Bishops' Committee on the Liturgy, National Conference of Catholic Bishops, *God's Mercy Endures Forever: Guidelines on the Presentation of Jews and Judaism in Catholic Preaching* (Washington: USCC, 1988) par. 8.

4. Vatican, "Guidelines" (1974) 2.

5. See Philip A. Cunningham, *Education for Shalom: Religion Textbooks and the Enhancement of the Catholic and Jewish Relationship* (Collegeville: The Liturgical Press, 1995). Each textbook reference to Jews or Judaism was rated as positive, negative, neutral, or ambiguous according to norms established in Catholic ecclesial documents issued since *Nostra Aetate*.

6. See Luke T. Johnson, "The New Testament's Anti-Jewish Slander and the Conventions of Ancient Polemic," *Journal of Biblical Literature* 108/3 (Fall 1989) 419–441.

7. For more information on New Testament anti-Jewish rhetoric see David P. Efroymson, Eugene Fisher, and Leon Klenicki, eds., *Within Context: Essays on Jews and Judaism in the New Testament* (Collegeville: The Liturgical Press, 1993).

8. Raymond E. Brown, *A Crucified Christ in Holy Week: Essays on the Four Gospel Passion Narratives* (Collegeville: The Liturgical Press, 1986) 11–12. For a detailed discussion of the trial of Jesus see his *The Gospel According to John, XIII–XXI*, The Anchor Bible (Garden City: Doubleday, 1970) 29A:791–802.

9. NCCB, *God's Mercy Endures Forever*, par. 21.

10. Note the comment in Sacred Congregation for the Sacraments and Divine Worship, *Introduction to the Lectionary for Mass*. 2d ed. (1981) 15: "Short and suitable introductions may be given before the readings, especially before the first. Careful consideration should be given to the literary style of these introductions. They should be simple, faithful to the text, short, carefully prepared, and should be varied to suit each text to be introduced."

11. Vatican, "Guidelines" (1974) 2.

12. As stated in Vatican Council II, *Dei Verbum* [The Dogmatic Constitution of Divine Revelation] (1965) 3:12: " . . . the interpreter of sacred Scriptures [in order to] ascertain what God has wished to communicate to us, should carefully search out the meaning that the sacred writers really had in mind." See also Pius XII, *Divino Afflante Spiritu* (1943) 23: "Let the interpreters bear in mind that their foremost and greatest endeavor should be to discern and define clearly that sense of the biblical words called literal . . . so that the mind of the author may be made clear."

13. As suggested by Pius XII: ". . . the interpreter must, as it were, go back wholly in spirit to those remote centuries of the East with the aid of history, archaeology, ethnology, and other sciences . . . which serve to make better known the mentality of the sacred writers, as well as their manner of art, reasoning, narrating and writing" [Ibid., 35, 40].

14. As recommended in NCCB, *God's Mercy Endures Forever*, 31-i: "Be free to draw on Jewish sources (rabbinic, medieval, and modern) in expounding the meaning of the Hebrew Scriptures and the apostolic writings. The 1974 *Guidelines* observe that 'the history of Judaism did not end with the destruction of Jerusalem, but went on to develop a religious tradition . . . rich in religious values.' The 1985 *Notes* (no. 14) thus speak of Christians 'profiting discerningly from the traditions of Jewish readings' of the sacred texts."

15. See Donald Juel, *Messianic Exegesis: Christological Interpretation of the Old Testament in Early Christianity* (Philadelphia: Fortress, 1988).

16. See the convincing study of Larry W. Hurtado, *One God, One Lord: Early Christian Devotion and Ancient Jewish Monotheism* (Philadelphia: Fortress, 1988).

17. Raymond E. Brown, *Jesus God and Man* (New York: Macmillan, 1967) 34–38.

18. Joseph Jensen, "Prediction-Fulfillment in the Bible and Liturgy," *Catholic Biblical Quarterly* 50/4 (October, 1988) 660.

19. Note the directive in Sacred Congregation for Divine Worship, *General Instruction of the Roman Missal* (1970) 73, that liturgical planners should address the "ritual, pastoral, and musical matters" of worship services. Such pastoral aspects could reasonably be seen to include Christian attitudes to Jews and Judaism.

20. The Gospel of Matthew provides a convenient example of this point. For that evangelist, in rivalry with nascent rabbinic Judaism, only Jesus can interpret the Torah definitively. See Daniel J. Harrington, *The Gospel of Matthew*. Sacra Pagina (Collegeville: Liturgical Press/Michael Glazier Books, 1991) 16–19; J. Andrew Overman, *Matthew's Gospel and Formative Judaism: The Social World of the Matthean Community* (Minneapolis: Fortress, 1990) 147–149.

21. In the words of one study, ". . . Christian beliefs are so deeply rooted in attitudes toward Judaism that it is impossible to disentangle what Christians say about Christ and the Church from what they say about Judaism." [Robert L. Wilken, *Judaism and the Early Christian Mind: A Study of Cyril of Alexandria's Exegesis and Theology* (New Haven: Yale University Press, 1971) 229.] For the impact of the patristic debate with Marcion on Christian attitudes to the Old Testament and to Jews, see David P. Efroymson, "The Patristic Connection," in *AntiSemitism and the Foundations of Christianity,* ed. Alan T. Davies (New York: Paulist, 1979) 98–117.

22. Vatican, "Guidelines" (1974) 2.

23. Vatican, "Notes" (1985) 2:7.

24. NCCB, *God's Mercy Endures Forever* (1988) 31-a, c.

25. See the judicious comments in Lawrence Boadt, *Reading the Old Testament: An Introduction* (New York/Mahwah: Paulist, 1984) 19–20.

26. Incidentally, the use of the term "Hebrew Scriptures" has been employed by John Paul II in his address "To the Jewish Community in Australia" (November 26, 1986) in Fisher and Klenicki, *John Paul II,* 95–97.

27. As correctly pointed out in Jensen, "Prediction-Fulfillment," 648–659. However, his safeguarding of the predictive aspects of biblical prophecy fails to reckon with such New Testament passages as the allusion in Matthew 2:14-15 to Hosea 11:1-4. No one could argue that Hosea was making any reference to the future in those verses. He was reflecting on the meaning of the past. Matthew's technique of making Hosea's words an anticipation of Christ is hardly responding to a prediction.

Thus, the issue is not simply that future hopes expressed by the Hebrew prophets were thought by later Christians to have been realized in Christ. Their re-reading of the prophets was far more complex.

In any case, as Jensen observes, the prediction-fulfillment reading of the OT "ought never to be used to encourage the idea that this is the only dimension that is of importance or interest to the Christian" (662). I submit that a methodology that respects both New Testament practice and modern critical understandings would seem to be demanded by the very nature of twentieth-century Catholic worship.

28. Vatican, "Guidelines" (1974) 2.

29. "Antitype" defined as that which is foreshadowed.

30. Vatican, "Notes" (1985) 2:8.

31. Ibid., 2:10-11.

32. NCCB, *God's Mercy Endures Forever*, 11.

33. See Sacred Congregation for Divine Worship, *General Norms for the Liturgical Year and the Calendar* (1970) 39: "Advent has a twofold character: as a season to prepare for Christmas when Christ's first coming to us is remembered; as a season when that remembrance directs the mind and heart to await Christ's Second Coming at the end of time."

34. E.g., John 9:22, used on the Fourth Sunday of Lent, Cycle A: "His parents answered in this fashion because they were afraid of the Jews, who had already agreed among themselves that anyone who acknowledged Jesus as the Messiah would be put out of the synagogue."

35. E.g., Acts 10:39, used on Easter Sunday: "We are witnesses to all that he did in the land of the Jews and in Jerusalem. They killed him finally, 'hanging him on a tree'. . . ."

36. E.g., Matthew 23:1-2, used on the Thirty-First Sunday in Ordinary Time, Cycle A: "The scribes and the Pharisees have succeeded Moses as teachers; therefore, do everything and observe everything they tell you. But do not follow their example. Their words are bold but their deeds are few."

37. Secretariat for Catholic-Jewish Relations, Bishops' Committee on Ecumenical and Interreligious Affairs, National Conference of Catholic Bishops, "Guidelines for Catholic-Jewish Relations," Recommended Programs (1967) 10e.

38. Note the axiom found in the Vatican, "Guidelines" (1974) 3, "Judaism in the time of Christ and the Apostles was a complex reality, embracing many different trends, many spiritual, religious, social, and cultural values."

39. NCCB, *God's Mercy Endures Forever* (1988) 19. See also the Secretariat for Catholic-Jewish Relations, NCCB; Adult Education Section, the Education Dept., USCC; and the Interfaith Affairs Department, Anti-Defamation League of B'nai B'rith, *Within Context: Guidelines for the Catechetical Presentation of Jews and Judaism in the New Testament* (Morristown, N.J.: Silver Burdett and Ginn, 1987) 4: "Certain of the conflicts between Jesus and 'the Pharisees' as depicted in the New Testament . . . may well reflect *internal* Pharisaic disputes, with Jesus siding with one 'side' against the other."

40. Vatican, "Notes" (1985) 3:17, 18.

41. Ibid., 21A.

42. See the Pontifical Biblical Commission's 1964 "Instruction on the

Historical Truth of the Gospels," presented in Joseph A. Fitzmyer, *A Christological Catechism: New Testament Answers* (New York/Ramsey: Paulist, 1982) 131–142. This document sketches the development of the Gospel traditions in three distinct time periods.

43. *Nostra Aetate* (1965) 4.

44. See Eugene J. Fisher, "Official Roman Catholic Teaching on Jews and Judaism: Commentary and Context," in *In Our Time: The Flowering of Jewish-Catholic Dialogue*, ed. Eugene J. Fisher and Leon Klenicki (New York/Mahwah: Paulist, 1990) 6–7.

45. NCCB, *God's Mercy Endures Forever* (1988) 25. See also the excellent pamphlet issued by the Bishops' Committee for Ecumenical and Interreligious Affairs, NCCB, *Criteria for the Evaluation of Dramatizations of the Passion* (Washington: USCC, 1988), which offers precise guidelines for any use of the Passion narratives.

46. John Paul II, "To the West German Jewish Community" (Nov. 17, 1980) in Fisher and Klenicki, *John Paul II*, 33–36.

47. Ibid.

48. Idem, "To American Jewish Leaders, *Origins* 17/15 (September 24, 1987) 241–243.

49. Idem, "To the West German Jewish Community" (November 17, 1980).

50. See the interesting article by Laurence Hull Stookey, "Marcion, Typology, and Lectionary Preaching" *Worship* 66/3 (May 1992) 251–262. The principles described in this introduction are in accord with what Stookey describes as a relationship of "complementarity" between the Jewish and Christian traditions (256).

51. Thanks, too, to Sr. Kathleen Haight, RCD, Mr. Stephen Nnakibinge Mukasa, and Dr. Barbara Anne Radtke for their helpful suggestions and questions.

1. Advent

CYCLE A

First Reading: Isaiah 2:1-5
All of this Advent's Hebrew Scripture readings are taken from the writings of Isaiah of Jerusalem, which comprise the first thirty-nine chapters of the book of Isaiah. This prophet was active during the time of the destruction of the northern kingdom of Israel by Assyria in 722 B.C.

In today's reading, Isaiah imagines how different the world will be when God's intentions for it have been fully realized. Not only will the present world of violence be replaced by a world of peace, but all humanity will walk by the Torah, or the teachings, of God.

Second Reading: Romans 13:11-14
In this portion of his final letter, that written to the Church in Rome, the Apostle Paul describes how believers should live as they await the coming of the Lord in glory.

Gospel: Matthew 24:37-44
Today's excerpt from Matthew's Gospel immediately follows a statement by Jesus that only the Father knows when the reign of God will be fully established. Not even the Son knows the day or the hour. All must be prepared for the Lord's coming at any moment.

CYCLE B

First Reading: Isaiah 63:16-17, 19; 64:2-7
In today's reading from the Hebrew Scriptures, the prophet known as
Isaiah of the Restoration prays to God for assistance as the newly re-
turned exiles from Babylon seek to rebuild their lives. Repeatedly ad-
dressing God as Father, the prophet hopes that God's presence will be
dramatically manifest, as it was on Mount Sinai centuries before.
Then, freed from sinful tendencies, the people will be like clay in
God's hands.

Second Reading: 1 Corinthians 1:3-9
In the following excerpt from one of his letters to the early Church in
Corinth, the Apostle Paul writes that God will fortify believers as
they wait for the return of Jesus in glory.

Gospel Reading: Mark 13:33-37
In today's reading from the Gospel of Mark, Jesus warns that God's
people must be prepared to demonstrate their faithfulness at all
times.

CYCLE C

First Reading: Jeremiah 33:14-16
In today's opening reading from the Hebrew Scriptures, the prophet
Jeremiah assures those Jews being exiled to Babylon that God has not
abandoned them. Land, Temple, and kingship will all be restored by
the just God of all.

Second Reading: 1 Thessalonians 3:12–4:2
The following reading is from the conclusion of Paul's letter to the
Church in Thessalonica. He encourages that early church, just as he
would encourage our own parish family, to continue to grow in the
Christian faith.

Gospel: Luke 21:25-28, 34-36
Today's Gospel passage is composed in a style of writing called apoca-
lyptic, in which vivid symbolism and catastrophic events dominate.
Since believers know that God's justice and peace must inevitably

prevail, we must strive to behave justly and peaceably even in the sinful world of the present.

SECOND SUNDAY OF ADVENT

CYCLE A

First Reading: Isaiah 11:1-10
Many of the Hebrew prophets felt that real peace could occur only in a society founded on justice. In today's first reading, Isaiah of Jerusalem anticipates how life would be under the rule of an ideal, totally just, king. The earth would be filled with "knowledge of the Lord." The Gentile nations would come to know the God of Israel.

Second Reading: Romans 15:4-9
The Apostle Paul believed that God was lavishing mercy upon the Gentile nations through his Son, the Lord Jesus. In this passage from the end of his letter to the Church in Rome, Paul states that Jesus' ministry to his fellow Jews led to the fulfillment of God's promises that pagans would one day know the God of Israel as the one, true God.

Gospel: Matthew 3:1-12
Today's Gospel gives us Matthew's portrayal of John the Baptizer. The baptizer, like Jesus, was a religious revivalist who urged his fellow Jews to change their minds and hearts and intensely commit their lives to God. Those halfhearted in their faith would be severely judged. The baptizer's words to the Pharisees and Sadducees challenge us today. Where is our evidence that *we* mean to reform?

CYCLE B

First Reading: Isaiah 40:1-5, 9-11
Today's reading from the Hebrew Scriptures is a moving prophecy proclaimed by Isaiah of the Exile. The prophet assures Jewish exiles in Babylon that God is about to pave a way through the desert so that

they will be able to return home again to beloved Jerusalem atop Mount Zion.

Second Reading: 2 Peter 3:8-14
In the following portion of the second letter of Peter, a Christian prophet, writing in Peter's name, encourages the Church community not to be anxious about the slowness with which God's kingdom is being established. While waiting for the coming of the Lord Jesus in glory, believers must be a holy and righteous people.

Gospel: Mark 1:1-8
In these opening words of the Gospel of Mark, the evangelist describes the mission of John the Baptizer with words that recall the message of Isaiah in our first reading. The baptizer is seen as one paving the way for the coming of Jesus. Relating this theme to our second reading, we could ask ourselves: Are we faithful disciples who are paving the way for the Lord's coming in glory?

CYCLE C

First Reading: Baruch 5:1-9
In today's first reading, the Jewish exiles in Babylon receive the best possible news. God, the God of justice, will lead the refugees back to their homes!

Second Reading: Philippians 1:4-6, 8-11
In this excerpt from Paul's letter to the Church in Philippi, the Apostle urges that community to live lives worthy of the kingdom of justice and peace which Christ will establish at his coming in glory.

Gospel: Luke 3:1-6
Today's Gospel passage echoes the sentiments of the first two readings: John the Baptizer announces that God is once more about to save the people. Therefore, they must recommit themselves to holiness.

THIRD SUNDAY OF ADVENT

CYCLE A

First Reading: Isaiah 35:1-6, 10
Today's Hebrew Scriptures reading offers another of the transcendent scenes envisioned by Isaiah of Jerusalem. When God brings the world to its completion, wastelands will blossom, physical ailments will be eliminated, and refugees will return home.

Second Reading: James 5:7-10
The Letter of James, attributed to James of Jerusalem, also known as "the brother of the Lord," has the expectation that Jesus, the Raised Lord, will return in judgment fairly soon. In today's excerpt from the letter, Christians are warned to live patient and upright lives.

Gospel: Matthew 11:2-11
In today's reading from Matthew's Gospel, John the Baptizer seems unsure of Jesus' mission and purposes. The reply of Jesus echoes the ideas of Isaiah of Jerusalem—the saving power of God is at work, bringing the world to its completion. The passage ends by contrasting followers of the baptizer with followers of Jesus.

CYCLE B

First Reading: Isaiah 61:1-2, 10-11
In the first of today's biblical readings, we again hear the words of Isaiah of the Restoration. The prophet rejoices that God has chosen him to announce marvelous news to those who had suffered Exile in Babylon. He praises God for acting to establish justice in the world.

Second Reading: 1 Thessalonians 5:16-24
In the conclusion of his letter to the Church in Thessalonica, the Apostle Paul prays that the community will abide in holiness and faithfulness as they wait for the coming of Jesus in glory. He adds that Jesus will indeed come to establish justice because God, the Trustworthy One, has said so.

Gospel Reading: John 1:6-8, 19-28
The Gospel of John is noted for its use of legal language. In today's passage from that Gospel, John the Baptizer gives "testimony" about his mission to prepare for the coming of the Lord. Do our lives give similar witness to our faith in the Coming One?

CYCLE C

First Reading: Zephaniah 3:14-18
All three of today's Scripture readings are filled with eager expectation. In the first reading from the prophet Zephaniah, the people of Judah are summoned to rejoice. God, the Savior of Israel, is about to rescue the holy city from hostile enemies!

Second Reading: Philippians 4:4-7
In this part of his letter to the Church in Philippi, the Apostle Paul urges the community to rejoice and be thankful. The Lord is coming soon to establish his reign of peace and justice!

Gospel: Luke 3:10-18
In today's Gospel passage, John the Baptizer eagerly announces the coming of God's kingdom of justice and peace. He urges his listeners to conduct themselves appropriately, to deal with one another with justice and amity.

FOURTH SUNDAY OF ADVENT

CYCLE A

First Reading: Isaiah 7:10-14
Our first reading today concerns an incident that occurred around 734 B.C. King Ahaz of Judah was fearful of being attacked by two neighboring kingdoms, but the prophet Isaiah of Jerusalem advised that the king had only to rely on God. He declared that before a newly conceived child had matured, the king's two enemies would have disappeared. Then the King would realize that the child had indeed been aptly named, "God is with us."

Second Reading: Romans 1:1-7
Today's second reading is the opening of the Apostle Paul's letter to the Church in Rome. Paul begins by observing that biblical promises of a Gospel of salvation for the Gentiles have become a reality through the raised Jesus.

Gospel: Matthew 1:18-24
Our Gospel reading today is a powerful section from the beginning of Matthew's Gospel. Matthew understands that with the coming of Jesus, Isaiah's certainty about the presence of God is more tangible than ever before. Through the child about to be born, God will be intimately and directly present among humanity.

CYCLE B

First Reading: 2 Samuel 7:1-5, 8-11, 16
Today's first reading describes an agreement called the "Davidic covenant." God promises that the dynasty of David, God's anointed, will endure forever. It eventually becomes clear, however, that this promise depends on whether the king will always be God's faithful servant by hearing the Word of God and carrying it out.

Second Reading: Romans 16:25-27
In the ending to his letter to the Church in Rome, the Apostle Paul praises God for bringing salvation, through Christ, to all the people of the world.

Gospel Reading: Luke 1:26-38
Today's Gospel reading comes from the infancy narrative of Luke's Gospel. Mary of Nazareth becomes the model of discipleship—she hears the Word of God and carries it out. Furthermore, the Davidic covenant is to be renewed by Jesus, the utterly faithful Son of the Most High.

CYCLE C

First Reading: Micah 5:1-4
Living at a time when the people of Israel were surrounded by foes and ruled by corrupt kings, the prophet Micah declared that a just

king would be called forth from Bethlehem, the hometown of the mighty King David. This passage reminds us Christians of Jesus, the shepherd king whose coming promises a reign of peace for the world.

Second Reading: Hebrews 10:5-10
For several weeks in October and November, we heard excerpts from the Letter to the Hebrews that was written after the destruction of the Temple in the year 70. This letter speaks of Jesus using the image of the high priest. Today's second reading returns to that theme, noting that, for Christians, Temple sacrifices are embodied in Jesus' sacrifice on the cross.

Gospel: Luke 1:39-45
The season of Advent draws toward its climax with today's Gospel reading. The final words of the passage are especially important for us today. Do we, like Mary, trust in the Lord's words to us?

2. Christmas

CHRISTMAS VIGIL

CYCLES A, B, C

First Reading: Isaiah 62:1-5
In today's Hebrew Scripture reading, the prophet Isaiah of the Restoration rejoices because the newly returned Jewish exiles from Babylon have rebuilt their Temple and their lives. The whole world can see how God saves the chosen people.

Second Reading: Acts 13:16-17, 22-25
The Acts of the Apostles, written by the author of the Gospel of Luke, contains many imaginative reconstructions of the sermons preached by the first apostles. In this passage, the Apostle Paul states that the coming of Jesus was part of God's covenant with the people of Israel.

Gospel: Matthew 1:1-25 or 1:18-25
[For the short form omit bracketed sentences.]
[For the evangelist Matthew, Jesus embodies in his own person the history of the chosen people. This is one point made in the genealogy with which Matthew begins his Gospel and which we hear today. In addition, . . .]

Matthew's infancy narrative highlights the righteousness of Joseph. Despite his worries, Joseph believes that through the child to be born, God will be present to the chosen people in a powerful and intimate way.

CHRISTMAS MASS AT MIDNIGHT

CYCLES A, B, C

First Reading: Isaiah 9:1-6
The prophet Isaiah of Jerusalem witnessed the gradual destruction of the northern kingdom of Israel seven hundred years before the time of Jesus. In this passage from his writings, he anticipates the birth of an outstanding king through whom God will restore Israel to its former glory.

Second Reading: Titus 2:11-14
The letter to Titus was written a few decades after the death of the Apostle Paul by a disciple who wrote in his name. In the following excerpt, the author declares that those who await the return of the Lord Jesus in glory must live as a chosen people should.

Gospel: Luke 2:1-14
Tonight's Gospel passage tells of the birth of Jesus during the reign of the Roman emperor Augustus. This Caesar had many monuments built in his honor, praising him as the provider of the Roman peace, whose birth was good news for the world. Tonight, however, Luke reveals that the true provider of peace is not to be found among the mighty, but among the poor.

CHRISTMAS MASS AT DAWN

CYCLES A, B, C

First Reading: Isaiah 62:11-12
Today's reading from the Hebrew Scriptures is a celebration of salvation. The prophet Isaiah of the Restoration rejoices because a second temple has been built after the destruction wrought by the Babylonians. God has brought new life to the chosen people.

Second Reading: Titus 3:4-7
The letter to Titus was written a few decades after the death of the Apostle Paul by a disciple who wrote in his name. In the following

excerpt, the author rejoices because, through Christ, God has given the gift of new life to the world.

Gospel: Luke 2:15-20
In this morning's Gospel passage, Luke shows us where God's new life is to be found—in a humble manger.

CHRISTMAS MASS DURING THE DAY

CYCLES A, B, C

First Reading: Isaiah 52:7-10
The prophet Isaiah of the Exile ministered to the Jewish refugees in Babylon during their captivity there. In the following reading from the Hebrew Scriptures, the prophet rejoices that he is the messenger who announces that God is about to restore destroyed Jerusalem. The nations will be in awe of this saving news!

Second Reading: Hebrews 1:1-6
In the Hebrew tradition, the wisdom of God was God's plan for creation through whom the world came into being. In this excerpt from the Letter to the Hebrews, an anonymous Christian writer speaks of Christ using wisdom imagery. Through Christ, we encounter God.

Gospel: John 1:1-18 or 1:1-5, 9-14
Today's Gospel passage comes from the opening of the Gospel of John and is a hymn in praise of the Word of God. The Word of God itself has come in the flesh to bring the love of God to humanity!

FEAST OF THE HOLY FAMILY

CYCLES A, B, C

First Reading: Sirach 3:2-6, 12-14
Today's first reading comes from a book in the Hebrew Scriptures that contains proverbial wisdom about proper living. In this excerpt, the sage praises loving respect for one's parents.

Second Reading: Colossians 3:12-21
It is widely agreed that the Letter to the Colossians was written by a disciple of Paul about a decade after the Apostle's death. This inspired disciple repeats Paul's teaching that forgiveness, love, and gratitude are basic elements of life in the Christian community. The writer also reflects the Greek culture of his time and describes the family in patriarchal ways.

CYCLE A

Gospel: Matthew 2:13-15, 19-23
Today's Gospel illustrates one of Matthew's favorite ways of thinking about Jesus. For Matthew, Jesus embodies in his own person the story of the chosen people. Like the infant Moses, his life is threatened by a wicked king. He will come up out of Egypt as the Israelites did during the Exodus. And in a word play on Nazirite/Nazorean, Jesus is called to holiness as are all God's people.

CYCLE B

Gospel: Luke 2:22-40 or 2:22, 39-40
[Short Form:]
Today's Gospel continues Luke's infancy narrative. Mary and Joseph are portrayed as pious and Torah-observant Jews who serve as holy models in Jesus' youth.

[Long Form:]
Today's Gospel continues Luke's infancy narrative. Mary and Joseph are portrayed as pious and Torah-observant Jews who serve as holy models in Jesus' youth. In addition, an aged prophet and prophetess express important insights about the child's destiny.

CYCLE C

Gospel: Luke 2:41-52
Today's reading from Luke's Gospel sheds light on the destiny of the young Jesus. His life is to be spent in the service of God, his Father.

SOLEMNITY OF THE EPIPHANY

CYCLES A, B, C

First Reading: Isaiah 60:1-6
In today's reading from the Hebrew Bible, Isaiah of the Restoration proclaims God's generosity to those returning from exile in Babylon. By bringing the exiles back home, all the nations of the world will witness God's glory. They will stream to Jerusalem to pay homage to the God of Israel and of the whole world.

Second Reading: Ephesians 3:2-3, 5-6
In this portion of his letter to the Ephesians, the writer explains that through Jesus, Gentiles have now become honorary members of God's people, along with the chosen people, the Jews. A saving relationship with God has now been extended to all the world, through Christ.

Gospel: Matthew 2:1-12
Magi were the royal counselors of the emperors of Persia and studied what today might be called "the occult." By describing the visit of three of these officials to Bethlehem, Matthew reveals that even pagan Gentiles are affected by Jesus' birth. Furthermore, the magi's gifts, items used at the burial of a king, suggest that the child's importance involves his death.

FEAST OF THE BAPTISM OF THE LORD

CYCLES A, B, C

First Reading: Isaiah 42:1-4, 6-7
Today's first reading comes from the writings of Isaiah of the Exile. The prophet declares to the Jewish exiles in Babylon that in addition to restoring them to their homes, God will also act through a chosen servant to bring justice even to the pagan nations.

Second Reading: Acts 10:34-38
In this portion of the Acts of the Apostles, Peter addresses the first Gentiles to enter the Church community. He affirms that God has

now acted, through Christ, to save all peoples. He also speaks of the beginnings of Jesus' ministry.

CYCLE A

Gospel: Matthew 3:13-17
The evangelist Matthew emphasizes that Jesus always observed the Torah and always did the will of God. In today's reading, taken from the opening pages of his Gospel, Matthew portrays both John and Jesus as obedient to the Father. Then the Holy Spirit anoints Jesus for the ministry that he is about to begin.

CYCLE B

Gospel: Mark 1:7-11
In this opening scene from Mark's Gospel, the evangelist portrays Jesus as anointed by the Spirit of God when John baptizes him in the Jordan. The ministry that Jesus is about to undertake is commissioned by God.

CYCLE C

Gospel: Luke 3:15-16, 21-22
The evangelist Luke often portrays Jesus as the model whom Christians must imitate. In today's passage from Luke's Gospel, the Holy Spirit anoints Jesus for the mission that he is about to begin. At our own baptisms, we assumed the same mission that Jesus began at the Jordan.

3. Lent

FIRST SUNDAY OF LENT

CYCLE A

First Reading: Genesis 2:7-9; 3:1-7
Among other things, the Eden story in the book of Genesis seeks to account for the existence of what is known in the Jewish tradition as the "yetzer ha rah," the inclination toward self-centeredness that permeates humanity. Even though fashioned in God's image to be lovingly oriented toward others, humanity's awareness of its limitations is linked to a grasping, selfish, un-Godlike lifestyle.

Second Reading: Romans 5:12-19 or 5:12, 17-19
For the Apostle Paul, Jesus' death on the cross is the ultimate expression of self-giving, the culmination of a life lived perfectly in God's image. Jesus shows how God always intended human beings to live. He shows how to overcome the human tendency toward self-centeredness.

Gospel: Matthew 4:1-11
As his ministry begins, Jesus struggles to remain true to his Father. His unswerving fidelity to God demonstrates the faithful sonship of Jesus and illustrates what it means to live in God's image.

CYCLE B

First Reading: Genesis 9:8-15
Today's Hebrew Scripture reading comes from the concluding verses
of the Flood saga in the book of Genesis. Recalling the image of a
warrior god with his bow and quiver of arrows, the God of Israel forever disavows the use of a destructive flood and hangs his bow in the
sky in token of this promise.

Second Reading: 1 Peter 3:18-22
In today's second reading, the author of the First Letter of Peter applies the saga of Noah and the Flood to the story of Jesus. The waters
of the Flood are compared with the waters of baptism through which
believers find their salvation.

Gospel: Mark 1:12-15
In this reading from the Gospel of Mark, Jesus, after his own baptism,
endures a testing and then begins his ministry of announcing salvation.

CYCLE C

First Reading: Deuteronomy 26:4-10
As we begin the season of Lent, today's Scripture passages are all
concerned with dedication to God.

In the first reading from the Hebrew Scriptures, Moses expresses
one of the central teachings of both Judaism and Christianity. Because
the people have been chosen to be God's own, they are obligated to
express their gratitude.

Second Reading: Romans 10:8-13
In this portion of his letter to the early Church in Rome, the Apostle
Paul instructs that because of God's boundless compassion, all who
turn their hearts toward the Lord will be saved.

Gospel: Luke 4:1-13
Today we hear of the "Temptation of Jesus" as recounted in Luke's
Gospel. Jesus provides a model for us all by resisting various entice-
ments because of his steadfast devotion to the Father.

SECOND SUNDAY OF LENT

CYCLE A

First Reading: Genesis 12:1-4
In this reading from the book of Genesis, we hear of the ancient beginnings of God's covenant with the Jewish people. God promises Abram that his Hebrew offspring will be the means through which God will bless all humanity.

Second Reading: 2 Timothy 1:8-10
This brief excerpt from Second Timothy reminds us that God also calls the Church to be a special and a holy people. However, we have not done anything to deserve such a blessing.

Gospel: Matthew 17:1-9
Composed many decades after Jesus' ministry, today's Gospel passage may have been used by early Christians to understand the meaning of Jesus' resurrection. God's raising of Jesus from death to radiant new life was seen as evidence that Jesus was an even more important figure than the legendary Moses and Elijah. As beloved Son, Jesus acts as God's chosen instrument for the furthering of God's designs for humanity.

CYCLE B

First Reading: Genesis 22:1-2, 9-13, 15-18
In this powerful incident from the book of Genesis, Abraham's love for his son Isaac is pitted against his love for God. In the end, God's love for Abraham proves to be the greatest of all.

Second Reading: Romans 8:31-34
In one of the most moving passages in all of his letters, the Apostle Paul writes of the surpassing depths of God's love. If God's own Son was given up for us, how great God's love for us must be!

Gospel: Mark 9:2-10
In the Transfiguration scene from Mark's Gospel, Peter, James, and John are dumbfounded by a transcendent experience. Out of the

midst of their awesome vision, they are commanded to heed the words of Jesus.

CYCLE C

First Reading: Genesis 15:5-12, 17-18
Today's first reading describes a ritual by which a covenant, or binding agreement, is enacted between God and Abram. In ancient Israel, parties entering into a solemn contract with one another would walk between the halved carcasses of animals as a way of saying, "may I be broken in two if I fail to abide by the agreement between us." The procession of the smoke and fire are signs of God's commitment to keep the promises just made to Abram.

Second Reading: Philippians 3:17–4:1 or 3:20–4:1
In this part of one of his letters, the Apostle Paul teaches that our covenant with God requires us to be devoted to the coming of the Lord in glory, and not to pursuits of fame or power or wealth.

Gospel: Luke 9:28-36
In today's reading from the Gospel of Luke, Peter, John, and James experience a vision of Jesus in transcendent glory. Luke's account stresses the continuity of Jesus with the Jewish tradition by having him speak to Moses and Elijah of his passage or "exodus" to Jerusalem. Through Jesus, the God of the covenant is acting once more!

THIRD SUNDAY OF LENT

CYCLE A

First Reading: Exodus 17:3-7
Today's first reading comes from the book of Exodus. During their trek from the oppression of Egypt to the freedom of God's promise, the people of Israel again experience God's life-giving concern for them.

Second Reading: Romans 5:1-2, 5-8
In his letter to the early Church in Rome, Paul recounts how God's
life-giving concern has brought sinful and godless Gentiles into the
love of God's Spirit. Through Christ's death, God's love has been
powerfully manifest.

Gospel: John 4:5-42 or 4:5-15, 19-26, 39-42
In this passage from the Gospel of John, Jesus is portrayed as the em-
bodiment of God's life-giving concern. After questioning Jesus about
three important issues in Samaritan theology, a Samaritan woman is
energized with new life. By evangelizing an entire town, she becomes
this Gospel's first Christian missionary.

CYCLE B

First Reading: Exodus 20:1-17 or Exodus 20:1-3, 7-8, 12-17
Today's reading from the Hebrew Scriptures is taken from the Book
of the Covenant section of the book of Exodus. The people of Israel
receive the teaching of the Lord, which instructs them how they, in
gratitude for their liberation from slavery, are to conduct their lives.

Second Reading: 1 Corinthians 1:22-25
In the following excerpt from his letter to the Church in Corinth, the
Apostle Paul explains that the crucified Christ embodies the self-giv-
ing wisdom of God.

Gospel: John 2:13-25
Unlike the other Gospels, the Gospel of John describes the distur-
bance caused by Jesus in the Temple at the beginning of his account.
In John's version, it is clear that the resurrection experience caused
Jesus' followers to think about him in ways which had been impossi-
ble for them earlier.

CYCLE C

First Reading: Exodus 3:1-8, 13-15
The Hebrew Bible reading for today is the pivotal scene in which God
calls Moses to liberate the Israelites from slavery in Egypt and in
which God discloses the divine name. The Hebrew words translated

as "I am who am," also mean "I will be who I will be." The God of
Israel is the God of limitless possibility. No unjust situation, no matter
how oppressive, can stand against the God of change and creativity.

Second Reading: 1 Corinthians 10:1-6, 10-12
In this part of his letter to the Church in Corinth, the Apostle Paul
refers to the story of Moses to warn against smugness among Christians. Being part of the saved community brings responsibility, not
privilege.

Gospel: Luke 13:1-9
Today's Gospel repeats the point made in the second reading. God is
patient, but wants believers to live reformed lives.

FOURTH SUNDAY OF LENT

CYCLE A

First Reading: 1 Samuel 16:1, 6-7, 10-13
In today's first reading, the prophet Samuel searches among God's
people for the next person to be king. He learns that God's choices do
not conform to superficial human expectations or prejudices. Is this a
lesson we need to learn as well?

Second Reading: Ephesians: 5:8-14
This portion of an early Christian letter instructs believers that God
desires behavior based on goodness and justice.

Gospel: John 9:1-41 or 9:1, 6-9, 13-17, 34-38
[Long Form:]
When the Gospel of John was written, sixty years after Jesus' ministry, Jewish members of John's church had recently been barred from
synagogue membership. This situation is evident in the comments
made about the parents of the blind man whom Jesus heals in this
Gospel passage. Angry at those who caused the expulsion, the Gospel
writer depicts the Pharisees as more blind than the formerly sightless
man. The anger in this passage should prompt us to reflect on times

when *we* have been blind, when we have failed to see God at work in unexpected people and places.

[Short Form:]
In this passage from John's Gospel, an unlikely figure, a blind beggar, becomes the sign of God's liberating presence. Are *we* prepared to recognize God's elusive presence in those who lie outside our definitions of decency and righteousness?

CYCLE B

First Reading: 2 Chronicles 36:14-17, 19-23
In the following portion of the book of Chronicles, the writer summarizes many centuries of Israelite history. It is apparent that the people's infidelity leads to disaster, but God's limitless, gracious mercy brings new hope out of despair.

Second Reading: Ephesians 2:4-10
In this excerpt from the letter to the Church in Ephesus, a disciple of Paul writes of God's generosity. Like the Israelites of old, we have been saved not because of any merit on our part, but because of God's gracious mercy.

Gospel: John 3:14-21
Today's reading from John's Gospel may have been shaped in a sermon given in the evangelist's early church community. That church felt alienated and spurned by the world, and, as is typical of such isolated groups, asserted that all outsiders were condemned. And so, this passage stresses not only that God's surpassing love caused Jesus to come into the world, but also that his coming confronts people with the choice to accept or reject his message.

CYCLE C

First Reading: Joshua 5:9-12
All of today's readings relate to the themes of God's generosity and providence.

The reading from the Hebrew Scriptures tells how God generously provided for the Hebrew people as they wandered in the desert and brought them safely to the Promised Land.

Second Reading: 2 Corinthians 5:17-21
In today's reading from Paul's letters, the Apostle stresses that God seeks universal reconciliation and unity.

Gospel: Luke 15:1-3, 11-32
God's constant and generous invitation to relationship is also the subject of the parable presented in today's Gospel reading. Be alert to the last sentence of the story: we are never told what the older brother decides to do. His decision rests with us who hear the story today. Will we be forgiving or judgmental?

FIFTH SUNDAY OF LENT

CYCLE A

First Reading: Ezekiel 37:12-14
To the Jewish contemporaries of Ezekiel, life seemed to have ended. The Temple of Solomon had been destroyed, Jerusalem had been ravaged, and many of the people exiled to Babylon. But the prophet declares that the God of Israel will restore the Israel of God back to life and to Land.

Second Reading: Romans 8:8-11
When Paul uses the word "flesh" he does not mean the skin or the body. He is referring to the tendency to sin and selfishness that pervades humanity. In Christ, the deathly corrosion of sin is replaced by the animating Spirit of God that raised Jesus from death.

Gospel: John 11:1-45 or 11:3-7, 20-27, 33-45
In a dramatic episode from the Gospel of John, Jesus embodies the life-giving power of God that transcends death itself.

CYCLE B

First Reading: Jeremiah 31:31-34
In today's reading from the Hebrew Scriptures, the prophet Jeremiah announces that God's covenant with Israel will be renewed. The

Torah, the teaching of the Lord, will become internalized in the people and woven into the very fabric of their being.

Second Reading: Hebrews 5:7-9
In this remarkable passage from the Letter to the Hebrews, the writer reflects on Jesus' agony when he was crucified.

Gospel: John 12:20-33
Today's reading from John's Gospel also considers the meaning of Jesus' crucifixion. Jesus' death is seen as necessary for the coming of new life.

CYCLE C

First Reading: Isaiah 43:16-21
In today's Hebrew Scripture reading, the prophet Isaiah of the Exile declares to the Jewish refugees in Babylon that God is about to cause a second Exodus. Just as centuries before the Israelites had been brought out of slavery in Egypt, so now God will bring the exiles out of Babylon.

Second Reading: Philippians 3:8-14
While writing to the Church in Philippi, the Apostle Paul speaks eloquently of his love for the risen Jesus. The life of the crucified and resurrected one inspires Paul in all that he does.

Gospel: John 8:1-11
In last week's Gospel, Jesus told a parable that called for forgiveness and not judgment. Today, an incident from Jesus' ministry is recounted that makes the same, perhaps shocking, point. Where do we stand on this issue? Should wrongdoers be punished or rehabilitated? Should they be ostracized or restored to community?

PASSION SUNDAY

The Procession with Palms

CYCLE A

Gospel: Matthew 21:1-11
In the following excerpt from the Gospel of Matthew, the evangelist portrays the entrance of Jesus into the holy city of Jerusalem. Jesus is depicted as a king who comes from the humble ranks of the common people.

CYCLE B

Gospel: Mark 11:1-10
As we begin our celebration of Holy Week, we hear from Mark's Gospel about Jesus' arrival in Jerusalem. He is hailed as the restorer of Israel's glory and prosperity.

or

Gospel: John 12:12-16
In John's Gospel, Jesus visits Jerusalem for various feasts on several occasions. In today's passage, however, his arrival in the holy city for the Passover provokes his public acclamation as a king.

CYCLE C

Gospel: Luke 19:28-40
Today, Luke tells of the end of Jesus' journey, or exodus, to Jerusalem. Recalling the angel's words to the shepherds at Jesus' birth, Jesus' disciples hail him as the bringer of peace.

PASSION SUNDAY

Mass

CYCLES A, B, C

First Reading: Isaiah 50:4-7
Our first reading comes from the second part of the book of Isaiah, which was written during the exile of the Jewish people in Babylon. The prophet urges those who are suffering at the hands of the Babylo-

nians to remain faithful to the God of the Covenant. The passage reminds us Christians of Jesus, who also remained faithful despite his own ordeal and suffering.

Second Reading: Philippians 2:6-11
The following reading is an early Christian hymn found in one of Paul's letters. The song praises Jesus for being supremely faithful to God, and praises God for exalting the faithful Jesus to lordship.

CYCLE A

Gospel: Matthew 26:14–27:66 or 27:11-54
Today's Gospel is from Matthew's passion narrative. Due to disputes with synagogues in his own time, Matthew charges a Jewish crowd with blood guilt for Jesus' death. We must be careful not to let Matthew's polemic lead us to wrong conclusions about the causes of the crucifixion. Jesus died because of the sins of all humanity.

To appreciate the narrative most fully, we should contrast the faithfulness of Jesus to God with our own failure to be as faithful. Our failure to promote the reign of God adequately means that Jesus is still being crucified in the flesh of the oppressed and victimized peoples of our twentieth-century world.

CYCLE B

Gospel: Mark 14:1–15:47 or 15:1-39
Today's Gospel is the passion narrative from the Gospel of Mark. Keep in mind that the chief priests, who figure prominently in the plot against Jesus, were appointed by Pontius Pilate and retained their positions of power at his pleasure. Pilate and the Temple authorities were in far greater collusion than the Gospels might suggest. The fact that Jesus was crucified as a pretender king with two other insurgents indicates that he was seen as a threat to Roman rule. His popularity with the Jewish people at large, which prompted his arrest in a secluded garden at night, only added to this perception.

Mark stresses that Jesus was utterly forsaken. His disciples desert him, one of them even flees naked in order to make his escape. Peter denies his friendship with Jesus with a curse, and Judas betrays him with an embrace. His final words on the cross are a scream of abandonment.

How faithful to Jesus are we? Do we abandon him when put to the test in our own lives?

CYCLE C

Gospel: Luke 22:14–23:56 or 23:1-49
Today's Gospel is the passion narrative from the Gospel of Luke. In hearing this account, it should be remembered that one of Luke's purposes in writing his Gospel was to assure Roman authorities that Christians were peaceful, law-abiding people who deserved legal recognition. The fact that the founder of Christianity was crucified on the orders of a Roman prefect is embarrassing to Luke. Therefore, he repeatedly stresses Jesus' innocence and tends to shift responsibility for Jesus' death onto Jewish figures.

Throughout his Gospel, Luke portrayed Jesus as the healing bringer of peace. This is also true in the passion narrative. Luke's is the only Gospel in which Jesus heals the ear that was severed during his arrest, in which Pilate and Herod become friends, in which Jesus prays for his executioners, and in which one of the criminals crucified with him repents.

This can lead us to ask ourselves, Do we bring healing and peace in our own lives? In times of violence and hatred, do we promote reconciliation and forgiveness even at the cost of personal risk?

HOLY THURSDAY

Chrism Mass

CYCLES A, B, C

First Reading: Isaiah 61:1-3, 6, 8-9
Today's first reading comes from the writings of Isaiah of the Restoration. This prophet ministered in the chaotic period after the Jewish refugees had returned to a land in ruins following their exile in Babylon. In this passage, the prophet reflects on the purposes of his ministry.

Second Reading: Revelation 1:5-8
Our second reading comes from the beginning of the book of Revelation. This work was composed during a period of terrible persecution

of the Church. In this excerpt, the writer assures his readers that the one who suffered crucifixion will return in triumph.

Gospel: Luke 4:16-21
In today's Gospel reading, the evangelist Luke applies the ideas of our first reading to the ministry of Jesus. In Jesus, the process of restoring the oppressed reaches a new height.

HOLY THURSDAY

Mass of the Lord's Supper

CYCLES A, B, C

First Reading: Exodus 12:1-8, 11-14
This passage from the book of Exodus describes how the Jewish people are to celebrate their release from bondage in Egypt. By annually partaking in this special Seder meal, the Jewish people commit themselves to promoting justice and freedom in the world because they are grateful to the just and liberating God who has redeemed them.

Second Reading: 1 Corinthians 11:23-26
Because Paul's letters were written about twenty years before the earliest Gospel was composed, the excerpt from First Corinthians that we are about to hear is the oldest reference to Jesus' Last Supper in the entire New Testament. Those who share the bread and the cup are committed to proclaiming the freedom and justice of the reign of God for which Jesus died.

Gospel: John 13:1-15
While the Last Supper scene in the Gospel of John makes no mention of bread and wine, it portrays Jesus as showing his friends how he wants them to live. They are to be one another's friends, rendering service and love to one another, even to the point of "laying down one's life for one's friends," as Jesus did.

GOOD FRIDAY

The Passion of the Lord

CYCLES A, B, C

First Reading: Isaiah 52:13–53:12
The first reading comes from the second part of the book of Isaiah, which was written during the Exile of the Jewish people in Babylon. The prophet describes the sufferings endured by a faithful servant in the Exile as the means through which the whole people, including the suffering one's descendants, will be blessed.

Second Reading: Hebrews 4:14-16; 5:7-9
In this portion of the Letter to the Hebrews, the writer conceives of Jesus' death according to the image of Isaiah's suffering servant of the Exile. Jesus' sufferings are seen as a source of blessing for all who follow him.

Gospel: John 18:1–19:42
The passion narrative from the Gospel of John is today's Gospel reading. Because John's church community, sixty years after Jesus' death, had been involved in a bitter struggle with the local synagogue community, the Gospel refers to "the Jews" in a hostile manner, almost as if Jesus and his disciples and his mother were not Jewish themselves. Despite this, the Gospel makes clear that the Romans and Pontius Pilate were those who executed Jesus.

Most importantly, this is the only Gospel which refers to "blood and water" flowing from Jesus. This is a symbolic way of saying that through Jesus' death the life-giving power of God's Spirit has been dynamically unleashed into the world. Jesus' death is the source of blessing for all humanity.

4. Easter

EASTER VIGIL

CYCLES A, B, C

Reading I: Genesis 1:1-2:2 or 1:1, 26-31
The beginning of the entire Bible, from which this reading is taken, describes the creation of the world by God. Everything is set into prescribed limits. Humanity, fashioned in God's likeness, is given responsibility for the world and its inhabitants.

Reading II: Genesis 22:1-18 or 22:1-2, 9, 10-13, 15-18
In this powerful incident from the book of Genesis, Abraham's love for his son Isaac is pitted against his love for God. In the end, God's love for Abraham proves to be the greatest of all.

Reading III: Exodus 14:15–15:1
The following excerpt from the book of Exodus describes an epic battle between the God of Israel and Pharaoh, the sun god of Egypt. Taking the side of oppressed slaves, the God of Israel is revealed as the champion of justice and freedom, against whom none can stand.

Reading IV: Isaiah 54:5-14
Isaiah of the Exile was a prophet to Jewish exiles who had been deported to Babylon following the destruction of Jerusalem in 586 B.C. In this passage from his writings, the prophet assures the traumatized refugees that their exile is not permanent because God's love for Israel is eternal and unshakable.

Reading V: Isaiah 55:1-11
In this selection from the writings of Isaiah of the Exile, the prophet praises the enduring faithfulness of God to the chosen people. God has declared that those who have been vanquished will be restored. Such a word, once spoken, will inevitably come to pass.

Reading VI: Baruch 3:9-15, 32–4:4
Lady Wisdom was a popular figure in the later writings of the Hebrew Scriptures. A feminine attribute of God, she is understood as God's divine plan for the world and its creation. In this reading, the prophet Baruch describes Lady Wisdom as the gift of the Torah or teaching that God gave to Israel. All God's people should pursue wisdom by seeking to follow all the teachings of the Lord.

Reading VII: Ezekiel 36:16-28
Ezekiel lived during the time of the conquest of Jerusalem by the Babylonians, and he prophesied to the Jews who were deported to Babylon. In this passage, the prophet assures the exiles that they will some day return home. On that day, the covenant with God would become part of their very beings and they would follow God's way perfectly.

Epistle: Romans 6:3-11
In this portion from his letter to the early Church in Rome, the Apostle Paul declares that all who follow Christ will be raised to new life just as Jesus was.

CYCLE A

Gospel: Matthew 28:1-10
Today's Gospel reading describes how the resurrection of Jesus first came to be perceived by his followers. Their discovery, though confusing, brings them peace.

CYCLE B

Gospel: Mark 16:1-8
The Gospel of Mark portrays the discovery of the empty tomb as a frightening event. This challenges us as well. Do we dare to believe that the Raised Jesus lives in our midst?

CYCLE C

Gospel: Luke 24:1-12
In this reading from the Gospel of Luke, the astonishing news of the resurrection is revealed. But it is news that is difficult to comprehend.

EASTER SUNDAY
Mass During the Day

CYCLES A, B, C

First Reading: Acts 10:34, 37-43
In this portion of the Acts of the Apostles, Peter proclaims to his fellow Jews that Jesus has been raised from death by God. Although executed by the Romans, Jesus will bring justice and forgiveness.

Second Reading: Colossians 3:1-4
Today's second reading comes from an early Christian letter. The author teaches that followers of Christ have died to sinful behaviors.

or

Second Reading: 1 Corinthians 5:6-8
In this excerpt from his letter to the Church in Corinth, the Apostle Paul declares that followers of Christ must put aside their former, sinful ways and put on the new life of the Raised One.

Gospel: John 20:1-9
Today's Gospel reading from John's Gospel describes the discovery of the empty tomb. The mysterious beloved disciple seems to grasp what has happened more readily than does Peter.

SECOND SUNDAY OF EASTER

CYCLE A

First Reading: Acts 2:42-47
Throughout most of the year the first reading comes from the Hebrew Scriptures, but during the Easter Season it is taken from the Acts of

the Apostles. That book is the second volume composed by the writer of the Gospel of Luke. It was written around the year 85, fifty years or so after the formation of the first church community in Jerusalem. Today's excerpt tells about that first church.

Second Reading: 1 Peter 1:3-9
For the next several weeks our second reading will come from the First Letter of Peter. It is uncertain whether Peter himself wrote this letter shortly before he died around the year 65, or if it was written in his name by disciples after his death. In either case, the letter contains important early Christian insights into the meaning of Jesus' death and resurrection. Today's passage teaches that belief in the resurrection of Jesus brings the promise of birth into a glorious new life.

Gospel: John 20:19-31
Today's Gospel reading, the story of doubting Thomas, is thought by many to be the original conclusion of the Gospel of John. If so, then the Gospel's final words pose a challenge to us—the Gospel's modern readers.

CYCLE B

First Reading: Acts 4:32-35
During the Easter Season our first reading is taken from the New Testament book known as the Acts of the Apostles. This work is the second volume composed by the author of the Gospel of Luke and was written around the year 85.

Today's excerpt describes a community so animated by the power of Easter that the social needs of all the Church's members are addressed.

Second Reading: 1 John 5:1-6
Throughout this year's Easter Season, our second reading comes from the First Letter of John. Written in the same church community that produced the Gospel of John, this letter was likely written a few years after the Gospel, around the year 100. It was probably composed to correct some former members of the community who were claiming that Jesus was a purely divine being and not really human at all. In today's passage the author insists that through Jesus' blood the love of God has conquered the world.

Gospel: John 20:19-31
Today's Gospel reading narrates the doubting Thomas story, which was probably the original conclusion of John's Gospel. Many feel that one of the Gospel's most important sentences is the last comment which Jesus speaks to Thomas; words which are addressed to us as well.

CYCLE C

First Reading: Acts 5:12-16
For the next few weeks our first reading, which usually comes from the Hebrew Scriptures, is taken instead from the Acts of the Apostles. This New Testament book is the companion volume to the Gospel of Luke and was written around the year 85. As is evident in today's passage, one of Luke's favorite themes is that the reconciling and healing power of Jesus lives in the family of the Church.

Second Reading: Revelation 1:9-13, 17-19
During this Easter Season, our second reading will come from the book of Revelation. This book was written around the year 95 during a persecution of Christians in Asia Minor by the Roman Emperor. Fearful of what could happen if his letter fell into Roman hands, the author, John of Patmos, wrote in a very symbolic style that only believers could easily understand. Due to this deliberate secrecy, the book of Revelation is often misinterpreted today. This passage presents a vision of the resurrected Jesus as one who will triumph over the evil forces that persecute the church.

Gospel: John 20:19-31
This Gospel reading is the original ending of the Gospel of John. In explaining why he wrote his Gospel, the author suggests to us that authentic faith is based not on seeing spectacular signs, but on believing the Word made flesh.

THIRD SUNDAY OF EASTER

CYCLE A

First Reading: Acts 2:14, 22-28
The reading we are about to hear from the Acts of the Apostles represents a sample of the earliest apostolic preaching about Jesus. Peter proclaims to his fellow Jews that God has raised Jesus of Nazareth from death because of his faithfulness.

Second Reading: 1 Peter 1:17-21
The following excerpt from the First Letter of Peter admonishes its readers to remember their responsibilities in Christ. Because they have been made holy by the shedding of Christ's blood, Christians have a duty to conduct themselves in a manner befitting sanctified people.

Gospel: Luke 24:13-35
Today's passage from Luke's Gospel recalls the mood of Jesus' friends after witnessing his execution. Filled with distress, the followers of Jesus are convinced that their movement has been crushed, even though they have heard rumors that Jesus has been raised. Perhaps reflecting the experience of the earliest Church, they learn that it is by sharing in the Lord's Supper that Jesus' living presence is perceived and celebrated.

CYCLE B

First Reading: Acts 3:13-15, 17-19
Today's scripture readings illustrate three different ways in which early Church communities tried to express their understanding of Easter.

In our first reading, Peter, the disciple who had denied Jesus three times, urges the people of Jerusalem to repent for any part they played in the death of the innocent Jesus. He declares that the Messiah's suffering unleashed the limitless, reconciling power of God in order that people's sins would be forgiven.

Second Reading: 1 John 2:1-5
Today's excerpt from the First Letter of John stresses the duty of those who claim to know the Lord Jesus. Since Jesus intercedes for our sins, we are under an obligation to obey Jesus' commandment of love.

Gospel: Luke 24:35-48
In today's Gospel passage, the disciples of Jesus become convinced that Jesus has indeed been raised to new life. Because of this realization, they begin to read the Hebrew Scriptures in new ways and to understand the resurrection as consistent with the Law and the Prophets.

CYCLE C

First Reading: Acts 5:27-32, 40-41
Today's first reading is a portion of the Acts of the Apostles. Although the preaching of the first apostles is warmly received by the people of Jerusalem, the high priest is displeased and arrests them. But after the intervention of a Pharisee named Gamaliel, a scene omitted in the following excerpt, the apostles are released and resume their preaching.

Second Reading: Revelation 5:11-14
In our second reading, John of Patmos continues his message of comfort to a terribly persecuted church. He describes a symbolic vision of great majesty as the heavenly court glorifies both God and the raised Jesus.

Gospel: John 21:1-19 or 21:1-14
The following passage is from a second ending added to the Gospel of John shortly after the completion of the original version. Although the mysterious "beloved disciple" recognizes the raised Jesus even before Peter, a moving reconciliation between Jesus and Peter takes place. Whereas Peter had denied Jesus three times, he now declares his love for him three times, and is commissioned to shepherd Jesus' flock in close imitation of Jesus.

FOURTH SUNDAY OF EASTER

CYCLE A

First Reading: Acts 2:14, 36-41
In today's first reading, the apostle Peter accuses his fellow Jews of complicity in the death of Jesus in order to prod them into accepting his message. Guilty of denying Jesus himself, Peter seeks to have his listeners repent and be baptized in Jesus' name into a renewed relationship with God.

Second Reading: 1 Peter 2:20-25
Our second reading, a portion of the letter attributed to Peter, is addressed to those who are in pain. Suffering believers are told to put their trust in the Shepherd who, in *his* time of suffering, trusted in God.

Gospel: John 10:1-10
Today's passage from the Gospel of John is thought by some to be a sample of the preaching heard in John's community. Jesus is pictured as a Good Shepherd who guides his sheep to safe pasture.

CYCLE B

First Reading: Acts 4:8-12
In today's excerpt from the Acts of the Apostles, Peter declares that by calling upon the name of Jesus, the healing and saving power of God is invoked. All those who rejected Jesus, starting with Peter himself, must be healed in Christ in order to be able to heal others.

Second Reading: 1 John 3:1-2
Our second reading discusses the greatness of God's love. By adopting us as children, God has gifted us with a destiny so glorious it cannot be fully comprehended.

Gospel: John 10:11-18
Today's portion of John's Gospel considers the willingness of Jesus to lay down his life. The author's church community, and scattered groups of Christians everywhere, are all under the guidance of Jesus' surpassing love.

CYCLE C

First Reading: Acts 13:14, 43-52
In today's reading from the Acts of the Apostles, Luke portrays a mixed reception to the preaching of Paul and Barnabas. Although "many Jews" are convinced by their words, other Jews oppose them and force them to move on. Thus the words of Simeon from early in Luke's Gospel come to fruition: Jesus is the occasion for the fall and rising of many in Israel.

Second Reading: Revelation 7:9, 14-17
In our second reading, John of Patmos continues his message of comfort to a terribly persecuted church. He describes the glorious destiny awaiting those whose faith remains strong even though they are subject to torture and death by the orders of the Roman Emperor.

Gospel: John 10:27-30
One of the themes of the Gospel of John is that believers must have a personal, intimate relationship with Jesus. This is conveyed by the images of a shepherd and his sheep in today's reading.

FIFTH SUNDAY OF EASTER

CYCLE A

First Reading: Acts 6:1-7
Our first reading describes a growing church. As the numbers of believers increase, it becomes necessary to organize various sorts of ministries to meet people's needs. In this particular instance, seven men with Greek names are chosen to see to the needs of Greek-speaking church members.

Second Reading: 1 Peter 2:4-9
In today's excerpt from the First Letter of Peter, the Church is described as a holy building built out of the lives of each of its members. With Christ as the keystone, all believers are to be a consecrated and priestly people.

Gospel: John 14:1-12
Today's Gospel passage, and those for the next several weeks, are taken from the Gospel of John's lengthy "Last Supper" discourse. In this excerpt, we learn that since Jesus does the work of the Father, Jesus' friends must be doing the Father's work also.

CYCLE B

First Reading: Acts 9:26-31
An overall purpose of the Acts of the Apostles is to illustrate the spread of the Church out from Jerusalem as far as Rome, the imperial capital of the known world. Today's passage introduces Paul, the apostle whom Acts portrays as the leading figure in the preaching of the Christian message to the Gentile nations.

Second Reading: 1 John 3:18-24
Continuing with our second reading's presentation of the First Letter of John, we learn today that our statements of faith are credible only if we live according to Jesus' commands.

Gospel: John 15:1-8
Today's passage from the Gospel of John stresses the need for a personal relationship with Jesus. The depth of that relationship will determine how well Christ's love is manifested in our lives.

CYCLE C

First Reading: Acts 14:21-27
In one of several summaries that appear in the Acts of the Apostles, Luke sums up the accomplishments of Paul and Barnabas as they end one of their missionary journeys and return to their base in Antioch. The spreading of the originally Jewish Church into Gentile lands is proceeding rapidly.

Second Reading: Revelation 21:1-5
Today's excerpt from the book of Revelation comes from near the end of that New Testament book. The visionary describes a picture of the final arrival of the reign of God in which all of the injustices and hurts of the present world are removed.

Gospel: John 13:31-35
The following passage is from the Last Supper scene in John's Gospel. In it, an essential characteristic of the Church is defined. How well does *our* community reflect this command of Jesus?

SIXTH SUNDAY OF EASTER

CYCLE A

First Reading: Acts 8:5-8, 14-17
Today's first reading is one of several New Testament passages that suggest that Samaria was one of the first places where preachers about Jesus from Jerusalem met with success. The action of the Holy Spirit was seen as evidence of divine blessing and guidance of these early missionary efforts.

Second Reading: 1 Peter 3:15-18
Today's portion of the First Letter of Peter repeats a theme we have encountered in previous weeks—suffering for faith in Jesus is not only an imitation of Jesus himself, it is also a way to God.

Gospel: John 14:15-21
In today's selection from the Last Supper discourse in the Gospel of John, Jesus promises to send a "Paraclete" to his followers. This Greek word is a legal term which means something like a "defense counsel," an advocate who will stand by the side of one accused. Even though Jesus is returning to the Father, the Spirit will guide his followers in truth and love.

CYCLE B

First Reading: Acts 10:25-26, 34-35, 44-48
Today's reading from the Acts of the Apostles presents a dramatic moment when it becomes clear that the Spirit of the Raised Lord has been given not only to Jesus' Jewish disciples, but to pagan Gentiles as well.

Second Reading: 1 John 4:7-10
Both today's second reading and Gospel were written in the same
early Christian community. The First Letter and Gospel of John both
emphasize that God's self-giving love is meant to be reflected in the
love uniting God's People.

Gospel: John 15:9-17
The Gospel of John echoes the thought just presented in the First
Letter of John by pointing out that Christians should love one another
the way Jesus has loved us. Like Jesus, we too should be willing to
lay down our lives for our friends.

CYCLE C

First Reading: Acts 15:1-2, 22-29
The Acts of the Apostles recounts one of the thorniest controversies to
face the young Church. Should pagan Gentiles joining the Jesus-
community be required to become Jews or not? Although probably
not realized at the time, the issue would determine whether the
Church would remain one variety of Judaism or would become a distinct religious community.

Second Reading: Revelation 21:10-14, 22-23
In today's reading from the book of Revelation, John of Patmos continues his visionary description of the ultimate establishment of the
reign of God in which good would triumph over evil. The recurrence
of the number twelve in the passage reflects the ancient view that
twelve was a special number that signified completion. Thus, the
heavenly city of God is shown to be cosmically complete.

Gospel: John 14:23-29
Today's reading from John's Gospel continues with excerpts from
Jesus' Last Supper address to his disciples. It conveys the evangelist's
belief that those who love as Jesus loves experience a mystical sharing
of divine life with the Father, the Son, and the Holy Spirit.

SEVENTH SUNDAY OF EASTER

CYCLE A

First Reading: Acts 1:12-14
In today's excerpt from the Acts of the Apostles, the women and men who compose the first church community gather in prayer while awaiting the coming of the promised Spirit.

Second Reading: 1 Peter 4:13-16
Continuing its discussion of the reality of suffering, the First Letter of Peter asserts that suffering for being a Christian is a way of praying, of glorifying God.

Gospel: John 17:1-11
In our Gospel passage from the Last Supper discourse in John's Gospel, Jesus prays for his friends. Just as Jesus glorified the Father by doing his assigned work, Jesus prays that his followers will glorify him by continuing the work that Jesus has assigned them to do.

CYCLE B

First Reading: Acts 1:15-17, 20-26
Continuing with its presentation of the growth of the early Church, today's reading from the Acts of the Apostles shows a concern for maintaining apostolic continuity with Jesus.

Second Reading: 1 John 4:11-16
The following portion of the First Letter of John refers both to God living in believers and also to those believers living in God. To share life with God, one must "abide in love"; or, in other words, one must obey Jesus' command to love one another.

Gospel: John 17:11-19
In today's Gospel passage, Jesus prays not only for his disciples, but also for us.

First Reading: Acts 7:55-60
In today's portion of the Acts of the Apostles, Luke recounts the death of Stephen. In Luke's first volume, his Gospel, Jesus had died with the words, "Father, into your hands I commend my spirit" and had prayed for the Father to forgive his executioners. In Acts, Stephen dies with similar words on his lips, thus providing another model of how Christians ought to face their deaths.

Second Reading: Revelation 22:12-14, 16-17, 20
Today's second reading concludes several weeks of excerpts from the book of Revelation by presenting the final verses of that New Testament book. The author, writing to churches that have been the victims of Roman oppression and torture, encourages his readers to remain steadfast in the faith. Jesus is coming soon to conquer the evildoers and to exalt the righteous.

Gospel: John 17:20-26
In this passage from John's Gospel, Jesus prays for his followers of both yesterday and today.

PENTECOST VIGIL

CYCLES A, B, C

First Reading: Genesis 11:1-9
With today's Vigil of Pentecost we resume the custom of selecting our first reading from the Hebrew Scriptures. This passage from Genesis recounts the chaos that occurs when people seek their own glory and fail to give glory to God.

or

First Reading: Exodus 19:3-8, 16-20
With today's Vigil of Pentecost we resume the custom of selecting our first reading from the Hebrew Scriptures. Today's passage from Exodus describes the meaning of the Jewish feast of Pentecost. It is a cele-

bration of the start of the Torah covenant between God and the People of Israel.

or

First Reading: Ezekiel 37:1-14
With today's Vigil of Pentecost, we resume the custom of selecting our first reading from the Hebrew Scriptures. This passage from the prophet Ezekiel recounts his experience of God during the Exile of Israel in Babylon. The creative power of the Spirit of God can restore even skeletons to vigor and life. The exiles will be restored.

or

First Reading: Joel 3:1-5
With today's Vigil of Pentecost we resume the custom of selecting our first reading from the Hebrew Scriptures. Today's reading comes from the book of the prophet Joel, which seems to date from the time after the Babylonian Exile. In this excerpt, the prophet dramatically recounts how the creative power of God's Spirit will affect the returning Jewish exiles.

Second Reading: Romans 8:22-27
In our second reading, Paul writes to the early Church in Rome that the coming of the Spirit is but a foretaste of the glory to come when all creation is made whole.

Gospel: John 7:37-39
In today's Gospel selection, Jesus declares that the coming of the Spirit will create a bubbling fountain of life in all believers.

PENTECOST SUNDAY

CYCLES A, B, C

First Reading: Acts 2:1-11
All three of today's Scripture readings examine the activities of the Holy Spirit, but from different points of view.

The Acts of the Apostles describes the descent of the Holy Spirit using imagery employed in the book of Exodus to depict the descent of God upon Mount Sinai. As a result of this divine manifestation, Jesus' followers are empowered to proclaim the Gospel with vigor and dynamism to all the nations.

Second Reading: 1 Corinthians 12:3-7, 12-13
In today's second reading, Paul teaches that each Christian is given different gifts by the Holy Spirit to be used for the betterment of the entire Church. The Spirit also brings a profound unity amid such great a diversity of gifts.

Gospel: John 20:19-23
The following passage from the Gospel of John reveals another consequence of the Spirit's presence. The Spirit empowers the Church to be a healing and reconciling presence in the world.

5. Ordinary Time

CYCLE A

First Reading: Isaiah 49:3, 5-6
In today's reading from the Hebrew Scriptures, Isaiah of the Exile
speaks about his call to be a prophet to the Jews exiled in Babylon.
Not only will the refugees be returned to Judah, but their restoration
will be a saving sign to all the nations of the world.

Second Reading: 1 Corinthians 1:1-3
In the opening words of one of his letters to the Church in Corinth,
the Apostle Paul greets the young community of Gentile believers by
reminding them that they have been called to be a holy people.

Gospel: John 1:29-34
In the following passage from the first chapter of John's Gospel, the
Baptizer testifies that Jesus has been sent by the Holy Spirit on a mis-
sion to Israel and to the world.

CYCLE B

First Reading: 1 Samuel 3:3-10, 19
Today's reading from the Hebrew Scriptures describes the call of the
prophet Samuel. He is to become one of those spokespersons for God
who speak God's word to the chosen people.

Second Reading: 1 Corinthians 6:13-15, 17-20
Today's second reading begins several weeks of excerpts from Paul's first letter to the Church in Corinth. In this portion, Paul warns the newly converted Gentiles that they must forsake their former practices. Among these behaviors was ritual prostitution at pagan temples. Paul admonishes the Corinthians that their own bodies are now "temples" that have been joined into the Body of Christ.

Gospel: John 1:35-42
Today's Gospel reading is the opening scene of John's Gospel. In it, those who are the first to encounter Jesus begin to spread the news that God's Anointed One has come.

CYCLE C

First Reading: Isaiah 62:1-5
In today's reading from the Hebrew Scriptures, we hear the words of Isaiah of the Restoration. The prophet declares God's unfailing love for the chosen people. They will be renewed and uplifted despite the calamities of the Exile that they have experienced.

Second Reading: 1 Corinthians 12:4-11
In today's second reading, the Apostle Paul declares God's unfailing love for the Church. Through the Holy Spirit, God calls forth various talents from among the faithful in order to build up the Christian community.

Gospel: John 2:1-12
Today's Gospel passage presents the "sign" performed by Jesus in Cana, an incident recounted only in the Gospel of John. Through his actions, Jesus produces an immense quantity of wine, symbolizing the long-awaited arrival of the reign of God. The scene's climax is found in the words of the head waiter: the choice wine, Jesus, has come at last!

THIRD SUNDAY IN ORDINARY TIME

CYCLE A

First Reading: Isaiah 8:23–9:3
In the late eighth century B.C., the prophet Isaiah of Jerusalem saw the gradual destruction of the northern kingdom of Israel by the empire of Assyria. In this passage, Isaiah declares that lands recently lost will not remain in darkness. God will defeat the invaders and restore these regions to the chosen people.

Second Reading: 1 Corinthians 1:10-13, 17
Learning that the Church in Corinth was divided into various factions, the Apostle Paul insists that to be Christian is to be unified. How well does *our* Christian community meet this standard?

Gospel: Matthew 4:12-23 [or 4:12-17]
As Matthew describes the beginnings of Jesus' mission, he takes note that Jesus ministered in Galilee. He recalls Isaiah's words that light would come to that region, and sees them enacted in the deeds of Jesus.

CYCLE B

First Reading: Jonah 3:1-5, 10
Today's reading from the Hebrew Scriptures comes from the parable about the prophet Jonah. Although he had initially resisted God's command to preach in the capital of the Assyrian Empire, Jonah now warns the city to repent.

Second Reading: 1 Corinthians 7:29-31
During his ministry as Apostle to the Gentiles, Paul traveled about in great haste in order to save as many pagans as possible before the return of the Lord in glory and judgment. In today's excerpt from First Corinthians, the Apostle teaches that people's lives should be completely focused on the New Age that is about to appear.

Gospel: Mark 1:14-20
In today's passage from Mark's Gospel, Jesus begins his ministry by announcing that the reign of God is coming. His message immediately attracts several Galilean fishermen.

CYCLE C

First Reading: Nehemiah 8:2-6, 8-10
Nehemiah was a governor appointed around 445 B.C. by the Persian emperor to reestablish the Jewish people after their exile in Babylon. Together with the priest, Ezra, he guided the construction of a second temple in Jerusalem. In today's first reading, Ezra urges the people to observe the Torah, the Law of God, with joy and gratitude, and not to weep over their past failures.

Second Reading: 1 Corinthians 12:12-30 or 12:12-14, 27
In this portion of a letter to the early believers in Corinth, the Apostle Paul compares the Church to the human body. All the various parts of the body are equal in dignity as members of the community, even though they have diverse functions to perform. All must be united if all are to be healthy.

Gospel: Luke 1:1-4; 4:14-21
Today's Gospel reading is taken from the opening chapters of Luke's Gospel. In it, we hear how Luke understands Jesus' ministry. Using the words of Isaiah of the Exile, the mission of Jesus is described as good news, especially for the oppressed.

FOURTH SUNDAY IN ORDINARY TIME

CYCLE A

First Reading: Zephaniah 2:3; 3:12-13
All of today's readings, in various ways, make the point that the God of Israel is on the side of the weak and humble.

In the Hebrew Bible reading, the prophet Zephaniah speaks to those soon to be conquered by the Babylonians. He stresses that if they humbly pursue justice, God will not abandon them.

Second Reading: 1 Corinthians 1:26-31
In this segment of his letter to Corinth, the Apostle Paul reminds his readers, and us, that believers have done nothing to merit God's grace. We must humbly remember that we have no reason to boast.

Gospel: Matthew 5:1-12
Today's reading from Matthew's Gospel presents an excerpt of the Sermon on the Mount. Like Moses on Mount Sinai, Jesus instructs how the people of God should behave. Those who humbly pursue justice will be vindicated by God.

CYCLE B

First Reading: Deuteronomy 18:15-20
As part of his farewell speech to the chosen people, Moses assures them that they will not be left without leadership. In this passage, the biblical definition of a prophet is apparent: A prophet is a man or woman who speaks on behalf of God to the people of Israel.

Second Reading: 1 Corinthians 7:32-35
In last week's portion of First Corinthians, we heard of Paul's conviction that the time before Jesus' return in glory was very short. This expectation is seen in today's reading as well. Because the Lord's second coming is so imminent, even married couples are challenged to turn their attentions from one another and to focus on the dawning of the New Age.

Gospel: Mark 1:21-28
In the opening chapter of his Gospel, Mark makes it clear that Jesus both speaks and acts with authority.

CYCLE C

First Reading: Jeremiah 1:4-5, 17-19
Today's Hebrew Scripture reading tells of the call of the prophet Jeremiah. Although as a prophet he will face opposition and danger, Jeremiah is assured that God will be with him.

Second Reading: 1 Corinthians 12:31–13:13 or 13:4-13
Continuing with his plea for unity in the Church in Corinth, the
Apostle Paul declares that every form of ministry, from the lowliest to
the most exalted, must all be founded on love.

Gospel: Luke 4:21-30
The evangelist Luke often portrays Jesus as the greatest of Israel's
prophets. This is true in the following reading in which Jesus, like
Jeremiah before him, encounters opposition from his kinfolk.

FIFTH SUNDAY IN ORDINARY TIME

CYCLE A

First Reading: Isaiah 58:7-10
During the Babylonian Exile, the prophet called Isaiah of the Exile
urged the Jewish refugees not to forget the Torah ethic that marked
them as God's people. Light would break into their darkness through
their actions.

Second Reading: 1 Corinthians 2:1-5
In addition to a divided community, the Apostle Paul was confronted
with other problems by the Church at Corinth. The following passage
from his letter to that church addresses people who used their ora-
torical skills to glorify themselves. In contrast, Paul stresses the weakness of the Crucified One.

Gospel: Matthew 5:13-16
As the Sermon on the Mount continues, Jesus, like Isaiah, reminds
both his fellow Jews and us that our actions should reflect the goodness of God.

CYCLE B

First Reading: Job 7:1-4, 6-7
The book of Job in the Hebrew Scriptures is one of the most profound
reflections ever written about why innocent people suffer evil. In

today's segment from that book, the horribly afflicted Job bemoans his sufferings.

Second Reading: 1 Corinthians 9:16-19, 22-23
Continuing with our readings from Paul's first letter to the Corinthians, the Apostle explains his policy of trying to save as many Gentiles as possible.

Gospel: Mark 1:29-39
As the Gospel of Mark unfolds, Jesus' reputation as a healer spreads. In these early chapters of Mark's Gospel, it seems that people seek Jesus out, not so much to hear his words, as to be healed.

CYCLE C

First Reading: Isaiah 6:1-8
All of today's Scripture readings involve the calling of certain people by God for special tasks. The Hebrew Scripture reading comes from Isaiah of Jerusalem. Isaiah describes the vision he had that convinced him that he was called to be God's spokesperson, God's prophet.

Second Reading: 1 Corinthians 15:1-11 [or 15:3-8]
This important passage from Paul's letter to the Church in Corinth is the oldest narrative about the resurrection in the New Testament. In it we hear about those called to be apostles, or messengers, of the raised Jesus, including Paul himself.

Gospel: Luke 5:1-11
Today's Gospel reading, from the opening chapters of Luke's Gospel, describes the calling of the first disciples of Jesus along the shores of the Sea of Galilee.

SIXTH SUNDAY IN ORDINARY TIME

CYCLE A

First Reading: Sirach 15:15-20
The book of Sirach is a collection of wise sayings and proverbs about virtuous living. In this portion, the sage declares to his fellow Jews that if they choose to observe the Torah, they will be following God's will.

Second Reading: 1 Corinthians 2:6-10
Continuing his discussion about true wisdom, the Apostle Paul observes that the Christian message of a crucified Lord appears foolish to those attracted by power and fame.

Gospel: Matthew 5:17-37 [or 5:20-22, 27-28, 33-34, 37]
Today's reading from Matthew's Gospel continues to present the Sermon on the Mount. As Moses taught the Torah on Mount Sinai, so, too, Jesus teaches an intensified Torah upon a mountain. In this passage, Jesus does not negate the Torah; he intensifies it in its own direction.

CYCLE B

First Reading: Leviticus 13:1-2, 44-46
Today's Hebrew Scripture reading describes the community health precautions to be taken to prevent the spread of leprosy.

Second Reading: 1 Corinthians 10:31–11:1
In this brief excerpt from one of his letters, the Apostle Paul urges all believers to be motivated by the desire to glorify God.

Gospel: Mark 1:40-45
In this passage from early in his Gospel, Mark describes how Jesus heals a leper and instructs him to follow the health codes of Leviticus. Despite an apparent effort to avoid sensationalism, the news of the cure attracts still more interest in Jesus.

CYCLE C

First Reading: Jeremiah 17:5-8
All of today's Scripture readings are concerned with trust in God. In this first reading from the Hebrew Scriptures, the prophet Jeremiah reminds us that only God is completely reliable.

Second Reading: 1 Corinthians 15:12, 16-20
In this part of his letter to the Church in Corinth, the Apostle Paul highlights the importance of trusting in the raising of Jesus from death. With our resurrection faith, we can trust that we too will be raised to new life.

Gospel: Luke 6:17, 20-26
Today's Gospel reading is Luke's version of a homily by Jesus that in Matthew is called the Sermon on the Mount. In Luke, however, this event occurs at a level place, and so could be called The Sermon on the Plain. In both accounts, Jesus blesses those who trust that the reign of God will come, sweeping away all evils and injustices.

SEVENTH SUNDAY IN ORDINARY TIME

CYCLE A

First Reading: Leviticus 19:1-2, 17-18
Today's Hebrew Bible reading is an important passage from the book of Leviticus, a volume written by Temple priests in order to promote ritual holiness. This passage reveals that true holiness requires love of others.

Second Reading: 1 Corinthians 3:16-23
In today's passage from First Corinthians, the Apostle Paul continues to combat the divisiveness in that early church community. He compares the whole community to a building constructed by God. Anyone who fragments that structure by forming factions is behaving according to the distorted wisdom of human society.

Gospel: Matthew 5:38-48
This week's Gospel passage continues to present the intensification of the Torah that was featured in last week's Gospel reading. Jesus first sharpens a commandment that was originally formulated to stop the violent escalation of tribal feuds into a total ban on retaliation for wrongs. The second rubric, "hate your enemy," is found nowhere in the Torah. But following Leviticus' train of thought, Jesus declares that even enemies must be loved.

CYCLE B

First Reading: Isaiah 43:18-19, 21-22, 24-25
The prophet Isaiah of the Exile had to persuade the disheartened Jewish refugees in Babylon to trust that God would rescue them. This message permeates today's first reading.

Second Reading: 2 Corinthians 1:18-22
Faithfulness is also the theme of this excerpt from Paul's letters. The Apostle teaches that the Christ was supremely faithful to God, and, through Christ, God is supremely faithful to the Church.

Gospel: Mark 2:1-12
In the past few weeks, Mark's Gospel has portrayed a gradually building popular frenzy over the cures performed by Jesus. The furor persists in today's reading, but the blasphemy accusation probably dates from the time of the evangelist when the divine status of Jesus was being debated by the Church and the Synagogue. In its original setting, the passage reveals a prime element of Jesus' preaching: the dawning reign of God brings *both* physical *and* moral healing.

CYCLE C

First Reading: 1 Samuel 26:2, 7-9, 12-13, 22-23
Today's Hebrew Scripture reading recounts an episode from the dynastic rivalry between King Saul and the future king David. Because of his reverence for the Lord's Chosen or Anointed One, in Hebrew *messiah*, David will not harm Saul when he has the chance.

Second Reading: 1 Corinthians 15:45-49
In this portion from the closing of his letter to the Church in Corinth, the Apostle Paul compares Jesus to Adam. Those baptized into Christ partake of a new source of life.

Gospel: Luke 6:27-38
Continuing with its presentation of the Sermon on the Plain, today's Gospel passage summarizes Jesus' preaching. Generosity, mercy, and love are the hallmarks of the new life demanded by Jesus.

EIGHTH SUNDAY IN ORDINARY TIME

CYCLE A

First Reading: Isaiah 49:14-15
In today's Hebrew Scripture reading, Isaiah vividly portrays God's love for the Jews exiled in Babylon.

Second Reading: 1 Corinthians 4:1-5
Sometimes, the letters of the Apostle Paul were written to respond to controversy or criticism. In this portion of First Corinthians, Paul answers faultfinders by asserting that God alone will be his judge.

Gospel: Matthew 6:24-34
Matthew's presentation of the Sermon on the Mount continues in today's Gospel reading. In the following sayings, Jesus urges a focus on God and not on material things.

CYCLE B

First Reading: Hosea 2:16-17, 21-22
The prophet Hosea preached in the northern kingdom of Israel about God's love for the chosen people using the metaphor of human spouses. In this reading, the prophet depicts the marriage of God and Israel being renewed by returning to the place where their "honeymoon" had occurred.

Second Reading: 2 Corinthians 3:1-6
In today's second reading, the Apostle Paul is apparently responding to critics who have produced letters of recommendation to prove that their teaching is more accurate than his. Paul replies that mere written words cannot match the evidence of the Spirit, whom the Corinthians have come to know because of Paul's ministry.

Gospel: Mark 2:18-22
The early chapters of Mark's Gospel provide more details about Jesus' healings than about his preaching. In this uncommon teaching passage, Jesus instructs that the coming of the reign of God requires new behaviors.

CYCLE C

First Reading: Sirach 27:4-7
The book of Sirach is a collection of proverbs about righteous living that was written around 175 B.C. The book is sometimes called *The Wisdom of Jesus Son of Sirach.* This passage discusses what one's words reveal about the speaker.

Second Reading: 1 Corinthians 15:54-58
As the Apostle Paul concludes one of his letters to the Church in Corinth, he rejoices in what God has done through Christ. Those who deserved death according to the Law have been rescued. This is because death itself has been rendered powerless through God's raising of Jesus to new life.

Gospel: Luke 6:39-45
Today's excerpt from the Sermon on the Plain in Luke's Gospel presents several sayings of Jesus about ethical living. A few are reminiscent of the proverbs of another Jesus, the son of Sirach from our first reading.

NINTH SUNDAY IN ORDINARY TIME

CYCLE A

First Reading: Deuteronomy 11:18, 26-28
The book of Deuteronomy in the Hebrew Scriptures stresses that those in covenant with God face a choice: to be faithful or disloyal to God. This is apparent in the following reading, which also makes reference to the phylacteries, worn by orthodox Jews to this day, which remind all Jews of their covenantal duties to God.

Second Reading: Romans 3:21-25, 28
Today we begin several weeks of excerpting Paul's letter to the Church in Rome for our second reading. This was the last of the letters that Paul himself wrote. It was probably written around the year 58 when Paul was planning to travel to Rome from Jerusalem in order to begin missionary work in the western half of the Roman Empire.

One of Paul's most strongly held convictions, apparent in today's passage, was that pagan Gentiles could become part of the Church without becoming Jews first. Through their faith in Christ, Gentiles could be saved without having to follow the Jewish Torah.

Gospel: Matthew 7:21-27
As the Sermon on the Mount draws to a close, Jesus emphasizes one of Matthew's favorite themes: the teachings of Jesus must be put into solid action.

CYCLE B

First Reading: Deuteronomy 5:12-15
One of the most remarkable practices of the ancient Hebrew people is discussed in today's first reading. Not only the chosen people, but even their slaves and domesticated animals, were to honor God by abstaining from physical labor on the Sabbath. This is because the God of Israel is the God who frees slaves from their drudgery.

Second Reading: 2 Corinthians 4:6-11
In this passage from one of the Corinthian letters, the Apostle Paul compares the present sufferings of the Church to the suffering of

Christ. While not yet glorified as Christ is, believers manifest the presence of the Crucified One through their own lives.

Gospel: Mark 2:23–3:6 [or 2:23-28]
In the time of Jesus, there were many debates among Jews regarding proper Sabbath observance. Some Pharisees, for example, may have argued that nothing physical at all should be done so that a person could focus on God without distraction. Other Pharisees appear to have held that helping others on the Sabbath was a way of honoring God. In this passage from Mark's Gospel, Jesus seems to argue one Pharisaic viewpoint against the other, although Mark has simplified the dispute for his Gentile readers.

CYCLE C

First Reading: 1 Kings 8:41-43
In today's Hebrew Scripture reading, King Solomon prays that the newly built Temple might lead pagan Gentiles to a knowledge of the one, true God.

Second Reading: Galatians 1:1-2, 6-10
Beginning today, and continuing for several weeks, our second reading will present portions of Paul's letter to the churches in Galatia. This is Paul's angriest letter. It seems to have been written around 54, just after Paul received news about Galatia that enraged him. From the letter's opening words, Paul's indignation is evident.

Gospel: Luke 7:1-10
A characteristic of both the Gospel of Luke and of the Acts of the Apostles is that Roman characters are always favorably portrayed. This is because of Luke's desire to have Christianity receive legal recognition by the Roman Empire. In today's passage, Luke presents a figure who may not have been rare in the first century: a Roman who admires Judaism and who becomes attracted to Jesus.

TENTH SUNDAY IN ORDINARY TIME

CYCLE A

First Reading: Hosea 6:3-6
Israel's ancient prophets stressed that religious rituals are meaningless without a sincere heart. Today's words from the prophet Hosea challenge us with the same idea: do our lives reflect love and knowledge of God or does lack of conviction turn our worship into meaningless routine?

Second Reading: Romans 4:18-25
In his letter to the Romans, the Apostle Paul refers to Abraham as a model for faith. Before the Torah had been given to Moses, Abraham had been blessed because of his faith in God. Now, through the faith of Christ, Gentile pagans can do the same, making Abraham the "father of many nations" indeed.

Gospel: Matthew 9:9-13
Today's Gospel reading highlights an essential feature of Jesus' ministry. He is especially concerned with those who have been marginalized from human society. Do we share this concern of Jesus in our lives today?

CYCLE B

First Reading: Genesis 3:9-15
Today's first reading from the book of Genesis describes the consequences of partaking of the tree of knowledge. There is a legendary explanation of why snakes wriggle on the ground and why humans seem to be instinctively repulsed by them. Far more importantly, the Man and the Woman become aware of their own limitations. Knowing they are weak, they seek to blame others for their actions.

Second Reading: 2 Corinthians 4:13–5:1
In this portion of one of his letters to the Church in Corinth, the Apostle Paul urges his readers not to be discouraged by their own weaknesses or by the difficulties of daily life. They should remember the glorious destiny that God is preparing for all of creation.

Gospel: Mark 3:20-35
In the time of Jesus there were two ways to account for persons who performed wonders and healings. Either God was with them, as with Moses, or they were allied with evil, demonic forces. In this passage, Jesus defends himself against the latter accusation. The idea of an "unforgivable sin" also appears in this reading. Such a notion seems odd since Jesus always stressed the limitless mercy of God. The severe language is probably a reply to foes who doubted that the Spirit of God was with the young Church.

CYCLE C

First Reading: 1 Kings 17:17-24
Our reading from the Hebrew Scriptures presents Elijah, the man of God. He is a person through whom God works in mighty ways.

Second Reading: Galatians 1:11-19
Continuing his angry defense of his apostolic authority, Paul declares that no human being has taught him the Gospel he preaches. It has come directly from God.

Gospel: Luke 7:11-17
In today's passage from Luke's Gospel, Jesus reminds us of Elijah. Like that ancient prophet, Jesus is also one through whom God works in mighty ways.

ELEVENTH SUNDAY IN ORDINARY TIME

CYCLE A

First Reading: Exodus 19:2-6
Today's Hebrew Scripture reading portrays how God acts to establish a formal covenant with the people of Israel.

Second Reading: Romans 5:6-11
Continuing with our presentation of Paul's Letter to the Romans, the Apostle describes how God has acted in Christ to save humanity.

Gospel: Matthew 9:36–10:8
In the following excerpt from Matthew's Gospel, Jesus acts to implement his ministry of renewing Israel's covenant by summoning and instructing the Twelve, symbols of the twelve tribes of ancient Israel.

CYCLE B

First Reading: Ezekiel 17:22-24
Ezekiel was a prophet in that period when Judah was conquered by the Babylonians, about six hundred years before the time of Jesus. In today's first reading, Ezekiel uses the metaphor of a great cedar tree to reassure the Jewish exiles.

Second Reading: 2 Corinthians 5:6-10
In our second reading, the Apostle Paul reminds the Church in Corinth that people will be held accountable for their lives. Those who walk in the faith of Christ ought to be confident that their lives will be pleasing to the Lord.

Gospel: Mark 4:26-34
Today's passage from Mark's Gospel presents two parables about the reign of God. The second parable recalls Ezekiel's cedar imagery. The ministry of Jesus, and our own ministries as Jesus' followers today, may appear to be of little consequence. But from such seemingly insignificant beginnings, the reign of God will come.

CYCLE C

First Reading: 2 Samuel 12:7-10, 13
All of today's Bible readings are concerned with the theme of forgiveness. In the Hebrew Scripture passage, David is remorseful for his sin of arranging the death of Bathsheba's husband, and he is forgiven by God. Nevertheless, his dynasty will be marked by division.

Second Reading: Galatians 2:16, 19-21
In today's portion of his letter to the churches in Galatia, the Apostle Paul reiterates a basic Jewish belief. No one can earn salvation by obeying commandments. Only by accepting God's forgiveness as an undeserved gift can one truly be saved.

Gospel: Luke 7:36–8:3 [or 7:36-50]
The Gospel of Luke stresses the healing and forgiving power of Jesus. In the following passage, Jesus embodies the reconciling mercy of God in both his teaching and his actions.

TWELFTH SUNDAY IN ORDINARY TIME

CYCLE A

First Reading: Jeremiah 20:10-13
The prophet Jeremiah was ridiculed and harassed by his contemporaries because of his unsettling proclamations. In this excerpt from the book attributed to him, Jeremiah bemoans his rejection but he trusts that the Lord will stand by him.

Second Reading: Romans 5:12-15
As his letter to the Church in Rome unfolds, the Apostle Paul compares Christ to Adam. Christ's selfless death offsets the selfishness of Adam.

Gospel: Matthew 10:26-33
In today's Gospel reading, Jesus instructs his disciples that they must not fear persecution. Like Jeremiah centuries before, they must instead place their lives in God's hands.

CYCLE B

First Reading: Job 38: 1, 8-11
Today's first reading comes from the final scenes of the book of Job. That book considers the problem of why evil befalls the innocent. In this passage, Job is reminded that it was God who fashioned the world by imposing order on primordial chaos as symbolized by the sea.

Second Reading: 2 Corinthians 5:14-17
In the following excerpt from one of Paul's letters to the Church in Corinth, the Apostle reflects on how God has recreated the world by raising Christ to new and glorious life.

Gospel: Mark 4:35-41
Today's Gospel reading portrays the creative power of God at work in Jesus. As herald and agent of the reign of God, Jesus continues the process of imposing divine order on chaos.

CYCLE C

First Reading: Zechariah 12:10-11
Today's Hebrew Scripture reading comes from the writings of a prophet who seems to have lived in the unsettled period after the Jewish exiles returned to Judea from Babylon. In this brief passage, the prophet declares that Jerusalem will see their behavior through God's eyes. Then the people will experience the grief that they have caused God.

Second Reading: Galatians 3:26-29
The following portion of Paul's Galatian letter is probably a very early hymn that was chanted while new Christians were being baptized.

Gospel: Luke 9:18-24
The Gospel of Luke reaches a significant turning point in today's Gospel reading. Jesus begins to tell his followers that he is destined to suffer and die.

THIRTEENTH SUNDAY IN ORDINARY TIME

CYCLE A

First Reading: 2 Kings 4:8-11, 14-16
The hospitality of a Shunammite woman toward the prophet Elisha is the topic of today's first reading. Acting on the advice of his servant, Gehazi, the prophet Elisha declares that her kindness will bring her a joyful blessing.

Second Reading: Romans 6:3-4, 8-11
The Letter to the Romans is the only letter Paul wrote to a church that he did not personally establish. The Roman Church was founded by

other apostles, probably from Jerusalem, who conveyed to the Gentile Roman believers a respect for the traditions of Judaism. In today's passage, Paul tells the Romans that their old, pagan lifestyles have been crucified with Christ. Now they must live the lives of people of God.

Gospel: Matthew 10:37-42
One of the ideas emphasized by the Gospel of Matthew is that the teaching of Jesus must be put into practice. In today's Gospel reading, neither the comforts of family life nor thoughts of self-advancement are to impede the implementation of Jesus' teaching. Moreover, hospitality must be extended even to the lowly.

CYCLE B

First Reading: Wisdom 1:13-15; 2:23-24
All three of today's scriptural readings are concerned with the presence of evil and injustice in the world.

The first reading from the Hebrew Scriptures insists that God is not the cause of evil and death.

Second Reading: 2 Corinthians 8:7-9, 13-15
In our second reading, the Apostle Paul instructs the Church in Corinth that believers have an obligation to share their goods with those who suffer the injustice of deprivation.

Gospel: 5:21-43 or 5:21-24, 35-43
In the Jewish tradition, the full arrival of the reign of God would mark the end of evil, war, and injustice in the world. In the following passage from Mark's Gospel, Jesus inaugurates the reign of God by beginning the elimination of disease and death.

CYCLE C

First Reading: 1 Kings 19:16, 19-21
Today's biblical readings all highlight the radical demands caused by following the Lord.

In the reading from the Hebrew Scriptures, Elisha is summoned to be the apprentice of the prophet Elijah. He must make a complete break with his past to do so.

Second Reading: Galatians 5:1, 13-18
In our second reading, the Apostle Paul writes to his Gentile converts that they must completely abandon their pagan pasts. Any pursuit of power, wealth, or dominance is a form of slavery that is contrary to the loving spirit of God.

Gospel: Luke 9:51-62
Today's Gospel passage emphasizes the need for a total commitment to the reign of God. Not only is Jesus himself so completely dedicated that he has no time to think of having a home or a place to rest, he expects his followers to be similarly zealous in their pursuit of God's reign.

FOURTEENTH SUNDAY IN ORDINARY TIME

CYCLE A

First Reading: Zechariah 9:9-10
Zechariah was a prophet in Judah following the return of the exiles from Babylon. In today's excerpt from his book, the prophet announces that the restored people, having been rescued by God, will not be ruled by a king who is a military hero, riding upon a warhorse, but by a monarch of peace who rides on a docile donkey.

Second Reading: Romans 8:9, 11-13
In the Letter to the Romans, Paul often contrasts "spirit" with "flesh." By doing this, he is not comparing the immaterial with the material, the body with the soul. Rather, "spirit" for Paul means a God-oriented life, while "flesh" means a sinful lifestyle. In today's reading, Paul encourages believers to live sinlessly in the world as befits those who follow the Raised Lord.

Gospel: Matthew 11:25-30
In today's Gospel passage, Matthew portrays Jesus using expressions from the Jewish tradition that were applied to the Wisdom of God.

For Matthew, Jesus is the Wisdom of God whose teachings bring rest and whose words make wise the simple.

CYCLE B

First Reading: Ezekiel 2:2-5
Today's reading from the Hebrew Scriptures is an excellent description of the role of a prophet. A prophet is a woman or man sent by God to confront the failures of God's people to live up to their covenantal obligations. The Hebrew prophets, and also prophets who may be called forth in the world today, challenge us to examine how well we fulfill the ethical duties of our covenant in Christ.

Second Reading: 2 Corinthians 12:7-10
In this excerpt from one of his letters, the Apostle Paul discusses some recurring physical ailment that afflicts him. He understands this disorder to be his share in the sufferings of Christ, demonstrating that God is most powerfully seen in great weakness.

Gospel: Mark 6:1-6
Today's Gospel reading depicts Jesus experiencing a typical reaction to a prophet. Those who have known the prophet before his or her call often cannot comprehend what is happening. Therefore, they reject the prophetic activities of their acquaintance.

CYCLE C

First Reading: Isaiah 66:10-14
Today's Scripture readings all express the idea that God can bring good things even out of tragedy.

In the reading from Hebrew Scriptures, the prophet Isaiah of the Restoration declares that Jerusalem, which had been destroyed by the Babylonians, will be renewed and the exiles in Babylon will be returned.

Second Reading: Galatians 6:14-18
In this portion of his letter to the Church in Galatia, the apostle Paul reflects on how a new creation has resulted from the horrible tragedy of Jesus' crucifixion.

Gospel: Luke 10:1-9 [or 10:1-12, 17-20]
Today's portion of Luke's Gospel recounts the sending forth of seventy-two disciples to proclaim the reign of God. Even though passing "in the midst of wolves," followers of Jesus are commissioned to bear witness to the values of the reign of God. That reign will come forth even from the present turmoil.

FIFTEENTH SUNDAY IN ORDINARY TIME

CYCLE A

First Reading: Isaiah 55:10-11
In today's first reading, Isaiah of the Exile declares that what God speaks must inevitably happen. The exiles in Babylon shall not be refugees forever because God has decreed otherwise.

Second Reading: Romans 8:18-23
In today's excerpt from Paul's Letter to the Romans, the apostle looks forward to the day when all of creation is brought to the completion intended by God. Believers must trust that this will come to pass because God has said it would.

Gospel: Matthew 13:1-23 [or 13:1-9]
Matthew's retelling of the parable of the sower is an excellent example of the main characteristic of a parable. Parables invite reflection because they contain unexpected or surprising elements. Imagine what Jesus' original listeners would have thought of the aim of the farmer in the tale and of the harvest produced at the story's end.

CYCLE B

First Reading: Amos 7:12-15
Today's Hebrew Scripture reading continues the discussion of biblical prophecy that began last week. In this passage, the prophet Amos asserts that he never asked to be a prophet, nor did he receive formal

training in prophecy. Like many prophets, he was engaged in other pursuits when he was summoned to be God's spokesperson.

Second Reading: Ephesians 1:3-14 or 3:1-10
For the next several weeks our second reading will come from the Letter to the Ephesians. This letter was probably written within a decade of Paul's death by a disciple who wished to continue Paul's teaching. In today's excerpt, the author reflects on the grandeur of God's eternal plan. God always intended to bring forth a saved people from the nations of the world through the death and raising of Christ.

Gospel: Mark 6:7-13
As the Gospel of Mark continues, Jesus sends forth the Twelve on a mission in the service of God's reign.

CYCLE C

First Reading: Deuteronomy 30:10-14
In today's Hebrew Scripture reading, an important quality of the Torah is discussed. God's teaching is not far away or hidden or abstract. It dwells within our hearts.

Second Reading: Colossians 1:15-20
For the next several weeks, our second reading will be taken from the letter to the Colossians. This letter was probably written around the year 70, a few years after the death of Paul, by a disciple who wished to perpetuate the teachings of his master. It contains profound, often mystical, insights into the nature of the Christian faith.

In today's excerpt, the author uses the Hebrew tradition of Lady Wisdom to describe Christ as the one who reveals God.

Gospel: Luke 10:25-37
In today's Gospel, Jesus and a lawyer have a friendly discussion about the Torah. The lawyer summarizes the Torah in typical rabbinic fashion by quoting from the books of Deuteronomy and Leviticus. In response to a further question, Jesus tells a story that develops an idea from Leviticus: everyone is my neighbor.

SIXTEENTH SUNDAY IN ORDINARY TIME

CYCLE A

First Reading: Wisdom 12:13, 16-19
The book of Wisdom is a collection of Jewish proverbial sayings about living a moral life. Today's portion of the book observes that God's power is surpassed only by God's benevolence.

Second Reading: Romans 8:26-27
In today's second reading, Paul reflects on the activity of the Holy Spirit. He notes that the Spirit empowers prayers to God which transcend human limitations.

Gospel: Matthew 13:24-43 [or 13:24-30]
[If long form used:]
Today's excerpts from the Gospel of Matthew are a series of parables about the reign of God. Despite small and contentious beginnings, the reign of God will inevitably transform the world as God intends.

[If short form used:]
Today's excerpt from the Gospel of Matthew is the parable of the grain and the weeds. Despite opposition and evil, the reign of God will inevitably come.

CYCLE B

First Reading: Jeremiah 23:1-6
The first reading today is a forceful declaration by the prophet Jeremiah. It is important both for ancient Israel and for God's people today. Those who are leaders in the community of God have a special responsibility for the people's welfare. God will replace those who abuse their authority with leaders who will be true shepherds.

Second Reading: Ephesians 2:13-18
In today's second reading, a disciple of the Apostle Paul considers how the blood of Christ brings unity.

Gospel: Mark 6:30-34
The following segment of Mark's Gospel describes a thoughtful moment in the ministry of Jesus. Then, as now, humanity searches for meaning and guidance.

CYCLE C

First Reading: Genesis 18:1-10
Today's first reading highlights the generous hospitality of Abraham. When three strangers appear, who will eventually be revealed as divine messengers, he offers them a snack. When they accept, Abraham races about and prepares a gourmet feast for them instead. The scene ends with surprising words.

Second Reading: Colossians 1:24-28
In today's excerpt from the Letter to the Colossians, a disciple of Paul reflects on a great mystery—through Christ, God has brought salvation to the Gentiles.

Gospel: Luke 10:38-42
In today's Gospel, Luke presents two sisters: Martha, who is striving to be hospitable, and Mary, who sits at Jesus' feet, listening to his words. In the ancient world, Mary's posture is the mark of a disciple.

SEVENTEENTH SUNDAY IN ORDINARY TIME

CYCLE A

First Reading: 1 Kings 3:5, 7-12
Today's Hebrew Scripture reading tells of the first days of the kingship of Solomon, son of David. Solomon's prayer to God demonstrates humility and a desire to govern according to God's will.

Second Reading: Romans 8:28-30
In the following brief passage from the Letter to the Romans, Paul praises God's timeless plan for the people that have been called into being as the Church.

Gospel: Matthew 13:44-52 [or 13:44-46]

[If long form used:]

Today's portion of the Gospel of Matthew again presents parables about the reign of God. Once perceived, the reign must be entered at all costs, and within the reign only justice will prevail. Note carefully the last sentence of the Gospel, which may be an autobiographical reference to the evangelist himself.

[If short form used:]

Today's portion of the Gospel of Matthew again presents parables about the reign of God. Once perceived, the reign must be entered at all costs.

CYCLE B

First Reading: 2 Kings 4:42-44

Our first reading today concerns the prophet Elisha. The power of God works through Elisha to bring relief to those suffering during a famine.

Second Reading: Ephesians 4:1-6

In a moving passage from the Letter to the Church in Ephesus, the author urges his readers to maintain the unity of the community by being humble and patient. The oneness of God ought to be reflected in the oneness of the Church.

Gospel: John 6:1-15

Although during this liturgical year most Gospel readings come from the Gospel of Mark, for the next several weeks excerpts from chapter six of the Gospel of John will be presented. Today's passage presents a scene reminiscent of Elisha in our first reading. The power of God is seen in the feeding of the multitudes by Jesus. As Christians today, we are similarly nourished for our mission in the world when we gather at the Eucharistic table of the Lord.

CYCLE C

First Reading: Genesis 18:20-32

Today's Hebrew Scripture reading is a wonderful example of the intimacy that is possible for those in covenant with God. Abraham negotiates with God about an issue of justice and their conversation flows back and forth between them. Abraham's confidence in the strength of his relationship with God is a model for all God's people.

Second Reading: Colossians 2:12-14
Our second reading continues to present the reflections of the writer of the Letter to the Colossians. He stresses how Gentile Christians have died to their pagan way of life by their baptisms into the death of Christ. They have been raised to new life through the resurrection.

Gospel: Luke 11:1-13
In today's selection from the Gospel of Luke, the evangelist has collected together a number of different sayings of Jesus about prayer. Luke's version of the Lord's Prayer stresses that the coming of the Kingdom involves forgiveness. The other sayings encourage prayer to the One who shares the Spirit with us.

EIGHTEENTH SUNDAY IN ORDINARY TIME

CYCLE A

First Reading: Isaiah 55:1-3
In today's first reading, Isaiah of the Exile comforts the dispossessed Jews with the message that God's covenant with them is everlasting. God will heal their sorrows and restore their lives.

Second Reading: Romans 8:35, 37-39
In one of his most beautiful passages, today's excerpt from Paul's Letter to the Romans echoes Isaiah's insistence that believers cannot be separated from God's covenantal love.

Gospel: Matthew 14:13-21
In the following episode from Matthew's Gospel, Jesus embodies God's concern for the people.

CYCLE B

First Reading: Exodus 16:2-4, 12-15
Today's Hebrew Scripture comes from the book of Exodus. After rescuing the Israelites from Egyptian slavery, God feeds the people in the desert with bread from heaven.

Second Reading: Ephesians 4:17, 20-24
As the Letter to the Ephesians continues, the author reminds his Gentile readers that they have been called to forsake their former, pagan lifestyles.

Gospel: John 6:24-35
The following passage from the Gospel of John may be an example of the sermons preached about Jesus in the early Johannine church. Jesus is described as the Bread from Heaven who brings eternal nourishment to his followers.

CYCLE C

First Reading: Ecclesiastes 1:2; 2:21-23
Today's first reading comes from a book in Hebrew Scripture that is rarely included in the lectionary cycles. The book of Ecclesiastes, written around 250 B.C., is a writing that is skeptical about pious religious proverbs. It particularly questions any theology that ignores the fact that, in life, the good and the wicked, the wise and the foolish, often suffer the same fate.

Second Reading: Colossians 3:1-5, 9-11
In today's portion of the Letter to the Colossians, the author encourages his readers to put aside ungodly behaviors and to focus instead on the new life of Christ.

Gospel: Luke 12:13-21
Echoing our first reading, the following portion of Luke's Gospel shows Jesus criticizing what today is called "materialism." The pursuit of wealth and possessions is not consistent with living the life of God.

NINETEENTH SUNDAY IN ORDINARY TIME

CYCLE A

First Reading: 1 Kings 19:9, 11-13
The first reading today concerns the prophet Elijah. Elijah is demoral-
ized after fleeing for his life from evil rulers, and is drawn to Mount
Horeb, another name for Mount Sinai. There he hides in a cave trying
to escape his prophetic calling. God uses various manifestations of
glory to entice Elijah out of his hiding place, succeeding at last with a
whispering voice.

Second Reading: Romans 9:1-5
Our series of excerpts from Paul's Letter to the Romans continues in
our second reading. Today a discouraged Paul wrestles with the question of why his fellow Jews are not attracted to the Gospel he
preaches. He begins by rejoicing in the ongoing covenant with God
that Jews share in as the chosen people.

Gospel: Matthew 14:22-33
In today's reading from Matthew's Gospel, the disciples of Jesus are
panic-stricken when they see him under dangerous circumstances.
Like God with Elijah long before, Jesus seeks to calm their fears.

CYCLE B

First Reading: 1 Kings 19:4-8
All of today's Bible readings discuss the nourishment that believers
need to remain steadfast in their faith.

In the reading from the Hebrew Scriptures, the prophet Elijah is
deeply depressed by his failure to reform the corrupt rule of King
Ahab and Queen Jezebel. God sustains Elijah in his despair and
guides him through the desert to a renewal of spirit at God's holy
mountain, Mount Sinai, referred to as Mount Horeb in this passage.

Second Reading: Ephesians 4:30–5:2
In his letter to the Church in Ephesus, a disciple of the Apostle Paul
writes about the sustaining presence of the Holy Spirit. The Spirit
supports believers in their efforts to live God-like lives.

Gospel: John 6:41-51
Today's Gospel reading continues to present the bread of life discourse from the Gospel of John. These words are probably examples of the kinds of sermons preached in a Christian church, at the end of the first century, that was engaged in a vigorous debate with the local synagogue about the importance of Jesus. Today's excerpt stresses that Jesus brings transforming nourishment to the hearts of those who believe.

CYCLE C

First Reading: Wisdom 18:6-9
The book of Wisdom was written in Greek, about one hundred years before Christ, by a Jew living in Alexandria. He wrote in order to fortify the faith of his fellow Jews living in the pagan world. In today's passage, the author reflects on how God acted to rescue the Israelites during the time of the Exodus.

Second Reading: Hebrews 11:1-2, 8-19 [or 11:1-2, 8-12]
Beginning today, our second reading for several weeks will excerpt the Letter to the Hebrews. This New Testament book was written by an unknown Christian author who used concepts from the Jewish tradition to describe the significance of Christ. In this reading, the writer presents Abraham as a model for faith in God.

Gospel: Luke 12:32-48 [or 12:35-40]
Today's reading from Luke's Gospel offers several sayings of Jesus which stress that God is acting to bring about the kingdom. Believers should ready themselves for its appearance at any moment.

TWENTIETH SUNDAY IN ORDINARY TIME

CYCLE A

First Reading: Isaiah 56:1-7
Today's first reading comes from a prophet in the Isaiah tradition who preached to Jews newly returned to the Holy Land after their

Exile in Babylon. This prophet had a universal outlook and proclaimed that pagans could also become part of God's people.

Second Reading: Romans 11:13-15, 29-32
Continuing the discussion begun in last week's second reading, the apostle Paul expresses the hope that his Gentile converts will live such righteous lives that his Jewish kinfolk will recognize God's presence in the Church. Since God's call is irrevocable, both Jews and Gentiles will inevitably realize that God's mercy has graced everyone.

Gospel: Matthew 15:21-28
In today's portion from Matthew's Gospel, a Gentile woman implores Jesus' aid. Jesus, at first, seems to hold such pagans in low esteem, but then responds to the woman's arguments with praise for her faith.

CYCLE B

First Reading: Proverbs 9:1-6
In the later Hebrew tradition, the figure of Lady Wisdom plays an important role. She is a feminine figure of God who is the essence of God in the created world, in the book of the Torah, in the Temple of Jerusalem, and in the people of Israel. In today's excerpt from the book of Proverbs, God invites her people to partake of a great banquet she has prepared.

Second Reading: Ephesians 5:15-20
In the New Testament, the Holy Spirit often parallels the activities of Lady Wisdom. In this passage from his letter to Ephesus, a disciple of the Apostle Paul reminds his readers that the Spirit of God guides believers to live God-like lives.

Gospel: John 6:51-58
In today's Gospel, the bread of life sermon continues. The evangelist was probably influenced by the traditions about Lady Wisdom when he speaks of Jesus bringing life from above. The life of which Jesus speaks is not simple, biological life. Those who consume Jesus share in the life of love that unites the Father and the Son.

CYCLE C

First Reading: Jeremiah 38:4-6, 8-10
All of today's Scripture readings are concerned with the personal costs that faithfulness to God can bring.

In our first reading, the prophet Jeremiah's life is jeopardized because of his unpopular warning to King Zedekiah that Jerusalem would soon be conquered by the Babylonians. Jeremiah continues his proclamation despite grave personal risk.

Second Reading: Hebrews 12:1-4
In the following excerpt from the Letter to the Hebrews, the anonymous author asks his readers to remember how Jesus remained faithful to his mission, even though that led to the Cross. Jesus' followers should do the same.

Gospel: Luke 12:49-53
Today's Gospel reading comments on the discord that the preaching of Jesus brings. Because some will agree with his message, and others disagree, conflict is unavoidable. This will ultimately bring Jesus to his *baptism of fire*, a New Testament allusion to the crucifixion.

TWENTY-FIRST SUNDAY IN ORDINARY TIME

CYCLE A

First Reading: Isaiah 22:15, 19-23
In today's reading from the Hebrew Scriptures, Isaiah of Jerusalem declares that a corrupt royal official will see his power transferred to a man who is faithful to the covenant.

Second Reading: Romans 11:33-36
In the following excerpt from the Letter to the Romans, Paul concludes his reflections on the place of Jews and Christians in God's plan. Paul praises God's mysterious thoughts, which are far beyond humanity's comprehension.

Gospel: Matthew 16:13-20
Matthew's version of the confession of Peter, today's Gospel passage, is unique among the Gospels. In it, Peter in effect becomes the chief rabbi of the Christian community. He is empowered to interpret authoritatively the teaching of Jesus.

CYCLE B

First Reading: Joshua 24:1-2, 15-18
In today's Hebrew Bible reading, the people of Israel pledge themselves to the one God. In gratitude for all God did for them, they bind themselves to the Lord's service.

Second Reading: Ephesians 5:21-32
Today's second reading provides an excellent illustration of Catholic teaching that the Bible is the Word of God, written by human beings. Since God works through human authors, the Bible is shaped by human cultural limitations and customs. The author of Ephesians, trying to promote proper conduct in the church community, draws upon the Greek, patriarchal family structure with which he is familiar. In our times, these words should not be taken as a divine sanctioning of ancient cultural practices, but as urging believers to put their lives at the service of one another, just as Christ gave his life for the Church.

Gospel: John 6:60-69
The writer of the Gospel of John was well aware that being faithful to God's Word is often a difficult task. He experienced loss of faith within his own church community. In today's passage from John's Gospel, Peter provides an example of fidelity in the midst of uncertainty.

CYCLE C

First Reading: Isaiah 66:18-21
In the following reading from the Hebrew Scriptures, the prophet Isaiah of the Restoration envisions that all peoples will come to faith in the God of Israel. The world will be stunned because of this unexpected turn of events.

Second Reading: Hebrews 12:5-7, 11-13
Continuing his discussion of the meaning of suffering, the unknown author of the Letter to the Hebrews uses contemporary Greek child-rearing practices to suggest that sometimes suffering can produce benefits.

Gospel: Luke 13:22-30
In today's excerpt from Luke's Gospel, Jesus teaches that some of those who might be expected to be part of God's reign will be excluded, while some of those whom no one would expect to be in the reign of God will be its charter members. What implications does this saying have for us?

TWENTY-SECOND SUNDAY IN ORDINARY TIME

CYCLE A

First Reading: Jeremiah 20:7-9
All of today's Scripture readings touch on the price of faithfulness. The first reading is one of the laments of the prophet Jeremiah. Jeremiah bemoans the usual fate of the Lord's prophets—they are rejected and derided as troublesome messengers of bad news. But Jeremiah is trapped. He cannot keep silent because the Word of the Lord consumes him from within.

Second Reading: Romans 12:1-2
As the Letter to the Romans unfolds, the apostle Paul suggests that living the life of faith may have its costs.

Gospel: Matthew 16:21-27
In today's portion of Matthew's Gospel, Jesus teaches that suffering is an unavoidable consequence of discipleship.

CYCLE B

First Reading: Deuteronomy 4:1-2, 6-8
Today's Hebrew Scripture reading praises the revealed Word of God in the Torah, the first five books of the Bible. Often translated as *Law*, the Torah is better understood as a book of teachings through which God becomes present to the chosen people. Recalling last week's reading from Joshua, it is important to realize that the people of Israel follow the Torah not to earn God's favor, but rather out of gratitude to the God who has already favored them. Similarly, we Christians try to follow the way of Jesus not to earn God's favor, but out of gratitude for having already been favored through Christ.

Second Reading: James 1:17-18, 21-22, 27
Today's second reading is from the Letter of James, a short epistle not often proclaimed at our Sunday liturgies. Written toward the end of the first century, it may be an updating of an earlier letter composed by James, the Jewish leader of the Church in Jerusalem. The writer claims that God's Word should dwell in the hearts of believers, transforming their behaviors and actions from within.

Gospel: Mark 7:1-8, 14-15, 21-23
The importance of the Torah in the life of Jesus is evident in today's Gospel passage. In Jesus' time, there were a variety of ways in which the Torah was interpreted. True to the Jewish tradition that God becomes present in the effort to understand and apply Torah teachings, Jesus engages in a debate with a certain type of Pharisee over how to properly live the Torah. His approach resembles the thought of a rival Pharisaic tradition.

CYCLE C

First Reading: Sirach 3:17-18, 20, 28-29
Our first reading comes from the book of the Wisdom of Jesus Son of Sirach, written about 200 years before Christ. The writer is a scholar of the Torah who reflects deeply on the nature of God's wisdom and the meaning of human life. In today's passage, the sage warns that the more one learns, the more aware of their own ignorance they should become.

Second Reading: Hebrews 12:18-19, 22-24
Today's second reading concludes our series of passages from the Letter to the Hebrews. In the following excerpt, from near the letter's end, the writer says that believers should not be frightened of the power of God, but should rejoice in being accounted part of God's people.

Gospel: Luke 14:1, 7-14
Just as our first reading discussed the need for humility of thought, in this Gospel passage Jesus speaks about the need for humility in action. Those who do not seek dominance and who uplift the downtrodden are truly living according to God's wisdom.

TWENTY-THIRD SUNDAY IN ORDINARY TIME

CYCLE A

First Reading: Ezekiel 33:7-9
All of today's Scripture passages discuss the mutual obligations that members of faith communities owe to one another. In the reading from the Hebrew Scriptures, the prophet Ezekiel learns that a prophet has a responsibility toward others in the covenant.

Second Reading: Romans 13:8-10
In today's excerpt from the Letter to the Romans, Paul quotes Leviticus 19:18 as a summary of the duties of covenantal life.

Gospel: Matthew 18:15-20
In chapter 18 of Matthew's Gospel, the evangelist outlines procedures to reconcile differences among members of the Matthean church community. Today's passage stresses that people should be excluded from the Church only as a last resort.

CYCLE B

First Reading: Isaiah 35:4-7
All of today's Bible passages can be understood as referring to the reign of God. This phrase means that God has a vision for the world which will inevitably become reality.

In the first reading, the prophet Isaiah of Jerusalem envisions a world in which the afflicted are restored and wastelands become fruitful.

Second Reading: James 2:1-5
Today's excerpt from the Letter of James speaks of the behavior that should characterize those who believe in the reign of God. In God's eyes all people are equal in dignity. The people of God should share this vision.

Gospel: Mark 7:31-37
In the following passage from Mark's Gospel, the restorative power of the reign of God begins to become a reality in the ministry of Jesus.

CYCLE C

First Reading: Wisdom 9:13-18
Similar to the book of Sirach from last week's readings, the book of Wisdom is an example of a type of biblical writing called Wisdom literature. Written around 100 B.C., today's excerpt echoes Sirach's call for humility. Because they are mortal, humans are automatically restricted in what they can know. Only revelations from God can provide sure guidance.

Second Reading: Philemon 1:9-10, 12, 17
Today's second reading comes from the shortest of Paul's epistles, the Letter to Philemon. It recounts how Paul converted a slave named Onesimus and how this slave was sent by Paul back to his master, Philemon. Paul urges Philemon to regard Onesimus not as a slave, but as a brother in Christ.

Gospel: Luke 14:25-33
In this passage of Luke's Gospel, several of Jesus' sayings about commitment to the reign of God are placed together in order to highlight

this point: a person's dedication to God must be a well-considered priority in his or her life.

TWENTY-FOURTH SUNDAY IN ORDINARY TIME

CYCLE A

First Reading: Sirach 27:30–28:7
The Wisdom of Jesus Son of Sirach contains many proverbial sayings of great worth. In our first reading's excerpt, the sage advises that those who have been called into the covenant by a merciful God have a duty to be merciful to one another.

Second Reading: Romans 14:7-9
In today's segment of his Letters to the Romans, Paul, an apostle and Pharisee, teaches that believers live the life of the Lord and are, therefore, responsible to him.

Gospel: Matthew 18:21-35
Today's portion of the Gospel of Matthew contains a parable that dramatizes the wisdom contained in our first reading from Sirach. It also describes how members of the Church should treat one another.

CYCLE B

First Reading: Isaiah 50:4-9
All of today's Bible readings are concerned with the difficult and laborious aspects of striving to be faithful to God.

In the Hebrew Scripture reading, Isaiah of the Exile prophesies that those Jews banished to Babylon must remain faithful by being confident that God will vindicate them.

Second Reading: James 2:14-18
Today's passage from the Letter of James reminds us that those who profess to have faith have an obligation to labor on behalf of that faith.

Gospel: Mark 8:27-35
Today's Gospel reading is a pivotal passage in the Gospel of Mark.
Jesus rejects a triumphal understanding of his ministry. Instead, Jesus
insists that those who strive to be faithful to God, including himself,
must be ready to suffer for their efforts.

CYCLE C

First Reading: Exodus 32:7-11, 13-14
All of today's Scripture readings discuss the boundless mercy of God.
In this first reading, the people of Israel have recently fashioned and
worshiped a golden calf. But the covenantal mercy of God prevails.

Second Reading: 1 Timothy 1:12-17
For the next several weeks, our second reading will be taken from the
First and Second Letters of Paul to Timothy. Although introduced as
being "of Paul," these letters are widely agreed to date from near the
end of the first century, three decades after Paul's death. Following
the custom of the time, the letters were written by a disciple of Paul
in order to honor and perpetuate the teachings of that apostle.

This excerpt describes how God mercifully called Paul to be the
Apostle to the Gentiles.

Gospel: Luke 15:1-32 or 15:1-10
In this passage from Luke's Gospel, Jesus defends his liberal attitude toward outcasts by telling parables about the magnitude of God's mercy.

TWENTY-FIFTH SUNDAY IN ORDINARY TIME

CYCLE A

First Reading: Isaiah 55:6-9
In today's first reading, Isaiah of the Restoration proclaims that God's
mercy is generous beyond human comprehension.

Second Reading: Philippians 1:20-24, 27
Beginning today, and continuing for the next few weeks, the second
reading will feature portions of Paul's Letter to the Philippians. The

letter is thought to have been written around the year 54 while Paul was imprisoned. In this passage, Paul wonders if he might die before the return of the Lord in glory, but he longs to continue his apostolic work.

Gospel: Matthew 20:1-16
Today's Gospel of Matthew passage contains a parable that discloses the dire economic situation at the time of Jesus. Farmers have lost their own lands and must hire themselves out as laborers on other people's farms. The story's surprising ending speaks of the generosity of God toward those who have sought the kingdom only recently.

CYCLE B

First Reading: Wisdom 2:12, 17-20
Today's Bible readings continue last week's discussion of the costs of faithfulness to God.

The Hebrew Scripture reading describes the fate intended for a "son of God," by which the author means any faithful Jew, who by living according to the covenant with God incurs the wrath of the wicked.

Second Reading: James 3:16–4:3
In today's excerpt, the author of the Letter to James continues to remind us of the obligations of discipleship. Members of the community of Christ must not seek prestige within the community, or power over one another, or be jealous of one another's gifts. God's way is one of mutuality and peace.

Gospel: Mark 9:30-37
Despite Jesus' repeated instructions that believers must be humble and ready to share his self-sacrificing fate, the disciples continue to vie for dominance among themselves. This passage challenges our *own* behavior. Are we motivated by desires for social status and prestige, or by a spirit of service to others?

CYCLE C

First Reading: Amos 8:4-7
Today's selection of Scripture readings all discuss, in diverse ways, how believers should relate to the world's political authorities and to

material wealth. In the first reading from the Hebrew Scriptures, the prophet Amos attacks wealthy rulers who use their power to cheat and oppress the poor. He forcefully condemns their greed.

Second Reading: 1 Timothy 2:1-8
In the second reading, a disciple of Paul, living under the threat of persecution from the Roman Empire, adopts a more amicable tone. He urges believers to pray for political leaders so that they govern justly and that the empire will be filled with God's peace.

Gospel: Luke 16:1-13
Today's Gospel reading features one of the most difficult to interpret of Jesus' parables. It may be best understood by noting that it is followed in the same chapter of Luke by the parable of the rich man and Lazarus, our Gospel reading for next week. A dishonest manager takes swift action to ensure his own future when faced with a crisis. Jesus suggests that believers should be similarly moved to take swift action because they, too, face a crisis—how to live out their faith in the world. Like the manager, they must decisively use the world's goods to ensure their futures. However, for believers, the only proper use of the world's resources, as seen in the parable about Lazarus, is to use them on behalf of the oppressed.

TWENTY-SIXTH SUNDAY IN ORDINARY TIME

CYCLE A

First Reading: Ezekiel 18:25-28
All of today's Scripture readings are concerned with the behavior required of the people of God. In the first reading, the prophet Ezekiel asserts that God's justice accurately measures human conduct.

Second Reading: Philippians 2:1-11
In an important section of his letter to the Philippians, Paul adapts a hymn sung by early Christians to teach that the followers of Jesus must manifest the same humility and faithfulness which characterized the life of Jesus.

Gospel: Matthew 21:28-32
In another parable from the Gospel of Matthew, Jesus illustrates that actions speak louder than words.

CYCLE B

First Reading: Numbers 11:25-29
All of today's Bible readings discuss aspects of the life of a faith community.

The Hebrew Scripture reading reminds us that God bestows gifts within the community as God wills. God's spirit is not restricted by our petty preferences or wishes.

Second Reading: James 5:1-6
Today's reading from the Letter of James is a prophetic indictment against those who are unjust and greedy. The community of Jesus must constantly examine its own behavior in terms of justice and care for the weak.

Gospel: Mark 9:38-43, 45, 47-48
The need for constant, personal self-assessment is a major feature of today's passage from the Gospel of Mark.

CYCLE C

First Reading: Amos 6:1, 4-7
In last week's first reading, the prophet Amos condemned the wealthy rulers in the kingdom of Israel for cheating and oppressing the poor. He continues his invective in the following passage, declaring that their wanton revelry while others go hungry will lead to their downfall.

Second Reading: 1 Timothy 6:11-16
Today's second reading comes from the conclusion of the First Letter to Timothy. In it, the author, a disciple of the deceased Paul, outlines the virtues required by faith.

Gospel: Luke 16:19-31
Today's Gospel reading presents the parable of the rich man and Lazarus, a story found only in Luke's Gospel. Following on the heels

of the parable of the dishonest manager, which we heard last week, this story tells of the fate of those who serve self and exploit others. The consistent message of the Bible, as represented by Amos, Abraham, Moses, and Jesus, is that God judges the extent of people's faith by their treatment of the weakest members of society.

TWENTY-SEVENTH SUNDAY IN ORDINARY TIME

CYCLE A

First Reading: Isaiah 5:1-7
In today's first reading, Isaiah of Jerusalem uses the metaphor of a vineyard to describe God's covenant with the people Israel. He warns the rulers of the people that their continued failure to promote justice will inevitably bring disaster.

Second Reading: Philippians 4:6-9
Our second reading continues presenting sections of Paul's letter to the Philippians. In today's segment, the Apostle instructs that peace comes through prayer and ethical living.

Gospel: Matthew 21:33-43
In today's passage from Matthew's Gospel, Jesus uses Isaiah's image of a vineyard to tell a parable. In it he accuses the Temple leadership of failing in their stewardship over God's people.

CYCLE B

First Reading: Genesis 2:18-24
The Hebrew tradition perceived the inherent equality between female and male in the sight of God, although this understanding was not fully realized in Israelite society. In this reading from the book of Genesis, God forms a partner out of the man's very being. Since both man and woman are animated by the breath of God and both are fashioned by God, they are drawn together in unity.

Second Reading: Hebrews 2:9-11
For the next seven weeks, our second reading will be taken from the Letter to the Hebrews. It was written by an unknown Christian writer in the last third of the first century and stresses the newness and perfection of the covenant established in Christ. Today's excerpt teaches that believers are the brothers and sisters of Jesus.

Gospel: Mark 10:2-16 [or 10:2-12]
In today's passage from Mark's Gospel, Jesus cites the book of Genesis in order to highlight the sacredness of marriage. In Jesus' society, only men could divorce their spouses, and women were often victimized by arbitrary dismissals by their husbands. Jesus insists that those who are married are united in a binding covenant.

CYCLE C

First Reading: Habakkuk 1:2-3; 2:2-4
Today's biblical readings present three different insights into the meaning of faith.

The first reading comes from the writings of a prophet who lived in the tumultuous times before Jerusalem was destroyed by the Babylonians in 586 B.C. The prophet, Habakkuk, begins by complaining that God is doing nothing about the rampant violence which is tearing apart Judahite society. God responds that the person of faith must trust in God's power over human history.

Second Reading: 2 Timothy 1:6-8, 13-14
In our second reading, a disciple of Paul reflects on another aspect of faith. Believers must recognize that their faith will at times cause them hardship.

Gospel: Luke 17:5-10
Today's Gospel account presents yet a third perspective on faith. Disciples of Jesus must realize that faith is not something that they have earned as a reward for being good disciples. Faith comes as a free, unmerited gift.

TWENTY-EIGHTH SUNDAY IN ORDINARY TIME

CYCLE A

First Reading: Isaiah 25:6-10
In today's reading from the Hebrew Scriptures, Isaiah of Jerusalem describes the great feast celebrating the enthronement of God as king on Mount Zion. Even death will fall before the power of God.

Second Reading: Philippians 4:12-14, 19-20
This week concludes the second reading's presentation of Paul's letter to the Philippians. The Apostle expresses faith that God will provide what the community needs.

Gospel: Matthew 22:1-14 [or 22:1-10]
[If short form is used:]
The parable of the guests invited to a feast is today's selection from Matthew's Gospel. The Great Feast will occur with or without those formally invited.

[If the long form is used:]
The parable of the guests invited to a feast is today's selection from Matthew's Gospel. The Great Feast will occur with or without those formally invited, but all present must act appropriately.

CYCLE B

First Reading: Wisdom 7:7-11
Today's first reading praises the pursuit of Lady Wisdom. Those who seek God's way before anything else will find authentic wealth.

Second Reading: Hebrews 4:12-13
In our second reading, the Word of God, which corresponds to Lady Wisdom in the first reading, is understood as able to penetrate people's hearts.

Gospel: Mark 10:17-30 [or 10:17-27]
In today's Gospel passage, Jesus speaks profound wisdom. He declares that attachments to material possessions prevent participation in the reign of God. However, with God's help an addiction to materialism can be overcome.

CYCLE C

First Reading: 2 Kings 5:14-17
In today's first reading, the prophet Elisha refuses to accept a gift from a pagan warlord who has just been cured of leprosy. Acceptance would imply that Elisha was responsible for the healing. Instead, the prophet wants gratitude directed where it belongs—to God.

Second Reading: 2 Timothy 2:8-13
In the following excerpt from a letter written in Paul's name, the author stresses the centrality of the resurrection for Christian faith. Because Christ was raised, Christians will also be raised.

Gospel: Luke 17:11-19
The first reading's stress on being grateful to God is also emphasized in today's Gospel. A second point is made as well: sometimes those outside our faith community are quicker to acknowledge God's goodness than we are.

TWENTY-NINTH SUNDAY IN ORDINARY TIME

CYCLE A

First Reading: Isaiah 45:1, 4-6
This week's excerpt from the book of Isaiah concerns Cyrus, king of Persia, whose conquest of the Babylonians permitted the exiled Jews to return home to Jerusalem. Even though a pagan, Cyrus is described as the Lord's "anointed," his "messiah," because he has been the unwitting agent of God's plans.

Second Reading: 1 Thessalonians 1:1-5
Beginning today and continuing for the next five weeks, the second reading will excerpt portions of Paul's first letter to the Thessalonians. This is the earliest of Paul's letters, written around the year 50, and is also the oldest book in the New Testament. The Church in Thessalonica may have been the first successful Gentile community established by Paul, and Paul is particularly fond of it, as his opening words show.

Gospel: Matthew 22:15-21
In today's Gospel reading, Jesus is asked about the tribute that Judeans must pay to the Roman Empire. His clever answer should be understood in the context of the Torah tradition, which insists that only God deserves tribute.

CYCLE B

First Reading: Isaiah 53:10-11
In the following passage from Isaiah of the Exile, the prophet comforts the Jewish refugees in Babylon by claiming that out of their suffering, symbolized by the plight of the "suffering servant," justification will come. For us Christians, the prophet's words provide insight into the mystery of Jesus' passion. He, too, was a servant whose suffering brought justification.

Second Reading: Hebrews 4:14-16
In today's portion of the Letter to the Hebrews, the author uses the image of the high priesthood to reflect on the meaning of Jesus' death. Because Jesus was tempted and suffered like all human beings, he understands the frailties of the human condition.

Gospel: Mark 10:35-45 [or 10:42-45]
In this important passage from the Gospel of Mark, Jesus corrects those who seek positions of prestige in the Christian community. Because Jesus gave his life in service, authentic Christian leadership is characterized by an attitude of service. Leadership that dominates is not authentically Christian.

CYCLE C

First Reading: Exodus 17:8-13
The following excerpt from the book of Exodus recounts an attack on the Hebrew people as they wandered in the desert after their escape from Egypt. Moses, the agent of God, inspires resistance to the attackers, but he requires the help of others as he dramatically reminds the Hebrews of their dependence on God.

Second Reading: 2 Timothy 3:14–4:2
Today's second reading presents insightful comments on the role of the Scriptures in the lives of believers.

Gospel: Luke 18:1-8
In the parable of the unjust judge, Jesus suggests that if even corrupt humans can eventually do the right thing, then how much more certain it is that *God* will provide true justice.

THIRTIETH SUNDAY IN ORDINARY TIME

CYCLE A

First Reading: Exodus 22:20-26
Today's first reading, from the Exodus "Book of the Covenant," illustrates the orientation of the whole Torah, the "Teaching of Moses." Because the people of Israel know what it is like to be victimized and oppressed, their society must be governed by the divine principles of justice and compassion.

Second Reading: 1 Thessalonians 1:5-10
Continuing with the opening passages of Paul's letter to the Thessalonians, the second reading praises that early Church for the example it has set. All of Greece is edified because the Thessalonians have turned away from pagan idols to worship the one true God.

Gospel: Matthew 22:34-40
In today's portion of Matthew's Gospel, Jesus summarizes the Torah's love for God's justice and compassion by quoting Deuteronomy 6:4 and Leviticus 19:18. By doing so, he echoes the teachings of a great Pharisee named Hillel. Passages like this have led some to suggest that many of the Gospel accounts of Jesus arguing with Pharisees may actually show Jesus participating in a debate among different Pharisaic schools over how to interpret the Torah.

CYCLE B

First Reading: Jeremiah 31:7-9
Today's first reading is a jubilant exclamation of the prophet Jeremiah to the Jewish exiles in Babylon. Because Israel is God's firstborn, the exiles will be recalled from their banishment and tears will give way to laughter.

Second Reading: Hebrews 5:1-6
In today's excerpt from the Letter to the Hebrews, the author continues his reflection on Jesus as the Son of God, appointed as high priest for the sake of all.

Gospel: Mark 10:46-52
In the following passage from Mark's Gospel, blindness gives way to sight because of the renewing presence of the reign of God.

CYCLE C

First Reading: Sirach 35:12-14, 16-18
Occasionally over the past several months, we have heard portions of the book of Sirach, a collection of proverbial sayings. Today, we are presented with an excerpt that discusses the evenhanded concern of God for all the people.

Second Reading: 2 Timothy 4:6-8, 16-18
Today's second reading is taken from the conclusion of the Second Letter to Timothy. The author, a disciple of the deceased Paul, recalls the Apostle's reliance on the justice and mercy of God.

Gospel: Luke 18:9-14
In today's Gospel reading, Jesus tells a parable aimed at honest, decent people who try to live as God wants. Modern-day churchgoers might correspond to this audience. We who are trying to do our best must avoid the constant temptation to think of ourselves as better than those whose religious commitment is not very obvious.

THIRTY-FIRST SUNDAY IN ORDINARY TIME

CYCLE A

First Reading: Malachi 1:14–2:2, 8-10
Today's first reading is from the prophet Malachi, whose name means "my messenger." Malachi lived when a second temple was built after the Exiles had returned from Babylon. He may have been a priest. He insists that priests must conduct the Temple sacrifices properly and

must administer true justice. Otherwise, their sacred office would become a scandal to the people of Israel.

Second Reading: 1 Thessalonians 2:7-9, 13
In today's excerpt from Paul's letter to the Thessalonians the Apostle recalls that when he was in Thessalonica he earned his own living and did not engage in religious huckstering. He feels that this helped persuade the Thessalonians that his message was indeed from God.

Gospel: Matthew 23:1-12
The words of Jesus in today's Gospel recall the rabbinic caution that self-serving religious piety is worthless: "everything you do must be done for the love of God." In this passage, we can hear Jesus echoing rabbinic condemnation of religious hypocrisy, but we also hear Matthew, writing fifty years later, arguing with a local synagogue about proper religious practice. This Gospel asks us to examine our own motives for religious observance.

CYCLE B

First Reading: Deuteronomy 6:2-6
Today's first reading contains the most important prayer in the Jewish tradition, the *Shema* (pronounced "shmah"). It is called this after its first word, "Hear" or "Listen," which in Hebrew is "shema." For Jews and Christians alike, this prayer is the foundation of our relationship with God.

Second Reading: Hebrews 7:23-28
Considering yet another aspect of Christ's high priesthood, the author of the Letter to the Hebrews realizes that because Christ lives in transcendent glory, the effects of his sacrifice endure forever. His sacrifice does not need to be repeated ever again.

Gospel: Mark 12:28-34
Today's Gospel passage presents a friendly discussion between Jesus and a scholar of the Law of Moses. Jesus stresses the central importance of the *Shema* and, like other Jews of his time, adds the injunction of Leviticus 19:18 to "love one's neighbor as oneself." The scholar and Jesus are delighted with one another's ideas.

CYCLE C

First Reading: Wisdom 11:22–12:1
Today's Hebrew Scripture reading is from the book of Wisdom. In this passage, the author reflects on the cosmic grandeur of God who sustains the existence of all things.

Second Reading: 2 Thessalonians 1:11–2:2
Paul's preaching about the imminent return of Jesus in glory seems to have so excited the Thessalonians that they were consumed with eagerness and anxiety. In this excerpt from a letter to them, Paul seeks to minimize their agitation.

Gospel: Luke 19:1-10
The episode in today's Gospel reading is found only in the Gospel of Luke. Zacchaeus is a rich tax collector who has an unusually vivid sense of the responsibility that his wealth brings. He illustrates how wrong stereotypical expectations can be.

THIRTY-SECOND SUNDAY IN ORDINARY TIME

CYCLE A

First Reading: Wisdom 6:12-16
The first reading, from the book of Wisdom, praises divine Wisdom who is poetically personified in feminine form. Elsewhere, Wisdom is described as "pitching her tent" among the people Israel and as physically expressed in the Torah, the teaching of Moses.

Second Reading: 1 Thessalonians 4:13-18 [or 4:13-14]
The Church in Thessalonica has become alarmed because believers have died before Christ's return in glory. They feared whether their premature deaths excluded their loved ones from salvation. In today's second reading, Paul comforts the Thessalonians with the following instruction.

Gospel: Matthew 25:1-13
In the parable of the wise and foolish bridesmaids, Jesus stresses the urgency of developing one's faith relationship with God.

First Reading: 1 Kings 17:10-16
Today's first reading presents an incident in the career of the prophet
Elijah that highlights the virtue of generosity. Often in the Bible, as in
life, it is the poorest who seem the most ready to share the little they
possess.

Second Reading: Hebrews 9:24-28
The theme of the priesthood of Jesus, as we have seen, recurs frequently in the Letter to the Hebrews. In today's excerpt, the writer
notes that because Jesus generously shed his own blood, he has entered into the glory of the heavenly temple of God's presence.

Gospel: Mark 12:38-44 [or 12:41-44]
Continuing the ideas of today's first reading, this Gospel passage jux-
taposes the status-seeking elite with the generous poor. This compari-
son challenges those who are affluent today to share their abundance
with the oppressed.

CYCLE C

First Reading: 2 Maccabees 7:1-2, 9-14
The books of the Maccabees describe a revolt of the Jewish people
against the oppressive rule of a Greek king around 165 B.C. The following passage tells of the heroic fidelity of a family of Jewish martyrs who refused to stop following the Torah as the Greek king had
ordered. These martyrs believed that God would raise the righteous
to life after death, an idea which originated among the Pharisees.

Second Reading: 2 Thessalonians 2:16–3:5
Today's second reading advises that threats to one's faith can best be
met by an even deeper reliance on God.

Gospel: Luke 20:27-38 or 20:27, 34-38
In the time of Jesus, the Sadducees, or the Temple aristocracy, rejected
the idea of an afterlife. The Pharisees, various groups of nonpriestly
students of the Torah, promoted the idea of the resurrection of the
dead. In this excerpt from Luke's Gospel, we see Jesus supporting the
ideas of the Pharisees against the criticisms of the Sadducees. He asserts that God's power transcends even death.

THIRTY-THIRD SUNDAY IN ORDINARY TIME

CYCLE A

First Reading: Proverbs 31:10-13, 19-20, 30-31
Today's first reading is from the books of Proverbs. This selection
sings the praises of faithful daughters of the covenant.

Second Reading: 1 Thessalonians 5:1-6
Today's second reading continues Paul's instructions to the Church in
Thessalonica. Even though Christ might be returning soon, believers
must not slacken in their efforts to live holy lives.

Gospel: Matthew 25:14-30 [or 25:14-15, 19-20]
In today's Gospel passage, Jesus tells a parable about faith. Echoing
one of Matthew's favorite themes, the story suggests that faith must
produce real consequences in the lives of believers.

CYCLE B

First Reading: Daniel 12:1-3
The book of Daniel was written during the oppressive reign of a
Greek king. This heir to part of the empire of Alexander the Great,
sought to eradicate Judaism and assimilate God's people into Greek
civilization. He ordered parents who observed the Torah when raising
their children to be publicly tortured to death. He went so far as to
place a statue of Zeus in the holy of holies in the Temple of Jerusalem.
The writer of the book of Daniel, consequently, assures the faithful
that good shall ultimately triumph over evil and that the faithful shall
be vindicated.

Second Reading: Hebrews 10:11-14, 18
In today's second reading, the writer of the Letter to the Hebrews
looks forward to the final victory of good over evil at the return in
glory of Christ the high priest.

Gospel: Mark 13:24-32
The Gospel of Mark may have been written in Rome during the persecution of Roman Christians by the emperor Nero. In the following

passage, the evangelist assures his tormented church that they will see the triumph of good over evil.

CYCLE C

First Reading: Malachi 3:19-20
All of today's biblical readings discuss the coming of the reign of God, although they do so from different perspectives.

In the first reading, the prophet Malachi proclaims that God will bring justice upon the earth.

Second Reading: 2 Thessalonians 3:7-12
In the enthusiasm after the resurrection, many of the first Christians believed that Jesus would return in glory and inaugurate God's reign *very* soon. Some were evidently so preoccupied with this expectation that they ceased to work and took no thought for the future at all. Today's second reading addresses this problem.

Gospel: Luke 21:5-19
Today's Gospel passage reflects the concerns of Christians around the year 70 who endured persecution and war as they tried to persevere in their faith. These Christians are assured that they will see the reign of God if they remain steadfast in their faith.

SOLEMNITY OF CHRIST THE KING

CYCLE A

First Reading: Ezekiel 34:11-12, 15-17
In today's first reading, the prophet Ezekiel evokes the image of a shepherd to portray God's relationship with the chosen people.

Second Reading: 1 Corinthians 15:20-26, 28
In an important passage from his first letter to the Church in Corinth, Paul describes how all things will find their final destiny in the one God, who will ultimately be everything to everyone.

Gospel: Matthew 25:31-46
In today's Gospel reading, Jesus tells a story which illustrates the type of behavior which God demands of those called to be God's own.

CYCLE B

First Reading: Daniel 7:13-14

As the Church's liturgical year draws to a close, we look forward to the ultimate commencement of the reign of God when peace and justice shall prevail and God's will shall be established over all creation.

Today's first reading has always reminded Christians of Jesus. In it, one suffering under the tyranny of a foreign king, anticipates the coming of God's favored one in glory and judgment.

Second Reading: Revelation 1:5-8

Today's second reading from the book of Revelation is based on the passage from Daniel that we just heard. The writer, suffering during a persecution by a Roman emperor, anticipates the coming of Christ in glory and judgment.

Gospel: John 18:33-37

Today's Gospel passage depicts Jesus before Pontius Pilate. As occurs elsewhere in the Gospel of John, there are polemical remarks made against "the Jews" because of disputes between the author and a local synagogue. More valuable for us is the passage's spiritual insight: Jesus is the king whom Pilate is about to crucify. He is not an earthly despot who demands tribute, but a servant-king who lays down his life for his subjects.

CYCLE C

First Reading: 2 Samuel 5:1-3

Our first reading is a short passage that narrates how David became king over all the tribes of Israel. His kingship, though, must be in accord with God's will.

Second Reading: Colossians 1:12-20

The Letter to the Colossians was written in Paul's name by a disciple who had a distinctly mystical approach to the Christian message. Using Jewish imagery about Lady Wisdom, he describes Christ as the one through whom all creation has come into being and been brought together.

Gospel: 23:35-43
Mockingly crucified by the Romans as "King of the Jews," the tortured Jesus reveals what true kingship is. He is not a dominating dictator, but one who shares in the pains and mortality of his people.

6. Feasts

SOLEMNITY OF THE IMMACULATE CONCEPTION
December 8

CYCLES A, B, C

First Reading: Genesis 3:9-15, 20
In this selection from the opening chapters of the book of Genesis, some of the consequences of the eating of fruit from the tree of knowledge are presented. The Man and the Woman suddenly become conscious of their frailty and vulnerability, and human antipathy for snakes appears. This enmity was seen in later tradition as symbolic of the constant human struggle against sin.

Second Reading: Ephesians 1:3-6, 11-12
In this part of the Letter to the Ephesians, the author praises God for acting in Christ to adopt believers as beloved children.

Gospel: Luke 1:26-38
Today's Gospel reading comes from the infancy narrative of Luke's Gospel. Mary of Nazareth becomes the model of discipleship; she hears the Word of God and carries it out.

SOLEMNITY OF MARY, MOTHER OF GOD
January 1

CYCLES A, B, C

First Reading: Numbers 6:22-27
Our reading from the Hebrew Scriptures today presents the priestly blessing from the book of Numbers.

Second Reading: Galatians 4:4-7
In this portion of his letter to the churches in Galatia, the Apostle Paul comments on the coming of Jesus. Through the birth of Christ, pagan Gentiles have been enabled to call God their Father.

Gospel: Luke 2:16-21
Today's Gospel reading comes from the infancy narrative in Luke's Gospel. Once again, Mary is portrayed as pondering God's actions in her life. Following the thought of today's first reading, the coming of Jesus is seen as a time of great blessing for the whole world.

THE PRESENTATION OF THE LORD

CYCLES A, B, C

First Reading: Malachi 3:1-4
Today's reading comes from the book of Malachi. This book was written not long after the Jews who had been exiled in Babylon had returned to Jerusalem and rebuilt the Temple there. The name Malachi means "my messenger," and in this passage we hear of a messenger who will purify the sons of Levi, the Temple priesthood, and thus ensure that the sacrifices offered in the rebuilt Temple will be pleasing to God. In the New Testament, this messenger is often associated with John the Baptizer.

Second Reading: Hebrews 2:14-18
In the following portion of the Letter to the Hebrews, the anonymous Christian author reminds his readers that Jesus saved humanity because

he shared fully in the human condition—he was tested, he suffered, and he died.

Gospel: Luke 2:22-40 [or 2:22-32]
The story of the presentation of the infant Jesus in the Temple, an episode found only in Luke, reveals much about Luke's understanding of Jesus. He is the one who will bring glory to Israel, who will bring about the fall and rise of many Israelites, and who will be a light to the Gentile nations.

SOLEMNITY OF THE ASCENSION

CYCLES A, B, C

First Reading: Acts 1:1-11
The first reading today is the opening passage from the Acts of the Apostles and describes Jesus' exaltation to the "right hand of the Father." It also promises the gift of the Holy Spirit who will guide the Church in preaching about Jesus "to the ends of the earth."

Second Reading: Ephesians 1:17-23
The second reading, a segment of an early Christian letter, teaches that the exaltation of Christ must be the source of Christian hope.

CYCLE A

Gospel: Matthew 28:16-20
Today's Gospel passage is the ending of the Gospel of Matthew. Writing around the year 85, the evangelist instructs his readers that the Church has a job to do while awaiting Jesus' return. While doing our Christian work, though, Jesus will be with us always, thus fulfilling

the promise made at the beginning of Matthew's Gospel that Jesus would be called Emmanuel, "God with us."

CYCLE B

Gospel: Mark 16:15-20
Today's Gospel reading comes from the longer supplemental ending of the Gospel of Mark. Probably added by a later editor who was influenced by the Gospels of Luke and John, the passage stresses that although Jesus has been exalted to the Father, his followers have a mission of preaching to fulfill.

CYCLE C

Gospel: Luke 24:46-53
Today's Gospel passage is the ending of the Gospel of Luke that parallels the scene recounted in today's first reading. The importance of being witnesses to the exalted Jesus throughout all the nations is repeated.

TRINITY SUNDAY

CYCLE A

First Reading: Exodus 34:4-6, 8-9
Today's first reading is one of the most significant passages in the book of Exodus. It is a summary of Israel's experience of God, containing several important Hebrew terms for which there are no direct English equivalents. The emphasis is on God's enduring faithfulness and love for the chosen people.

Second Reading: 2 Corinthians 13:11-13
In the following conclusion to one of Paul's letters appears one of the earliest trinitarian expressions to be found in the Christian tradition. Paul exhorts the Church in Corinth to live in fellowship and peace, and thereby enjoy the life of God.

Gospel: John 3:16-18
The following passage from the Gospel of John declares that love was
the reason for God's Son to come into the world. Due to the isolated
and ostracized sentiments of John's church, the reading also condemns outsiders who do not believe in the Gospel, but this unhappy
attitude should not diminish the episode's main point: God loves the
world!

CYCLE B

First Reading: Deuteronomy 4:32-34, 39-40
Today's first reading comes from the book of Deuteronomy. In this
book, Moses is presented as giving a final speech to the people Israel
as they are about to enter the Promised Land. He stresses that God
has done wonderful things in forming Israel into a new people. Consequently, the people must show their gratitude by living according
to God's instructions.

Second Reading: Romans 8:14-17
In the following portion of his letter to the early church in Rome, the
Apostle Paul applies the Hebrew belief that Israel is God's son to the
new community of Christ. Those pagans whom Paul has converted
have become God's adopted children by being graced with the Spirit
of God.

Gospel: Matthew 28:16-20
Today's Gospel passage is the conclusion of the Gospel of Matthew.
The followers of Jesus are instructed to bear witness to their faith and
to baptize on behalf of the Father, the Son, and the Spirit. Jesus also
promises to be with the Church always, thereby fulfilling the words
at the beginning of Matthew's Gospel that Jesus would be known as
"Emmanuel," God with us.

CYCLE C

First Reading: Proverbs 8:22-31
Today's reading from the Hebrew Scriptures is a beautiful passage
about Lady Wisdom. A feminine persona of God, she informs much

of the New Testament's ideas about the Holy Spirit. Among other things, she is the guiding presence of God in the book of the Torah, in the Temple of Jerusalem, and in the people of Israel. In today's portion of the book of Proverbs, Lady Wisdom is God's playful partner in the creation of the world.

Second Reading: Romans 5:1-5
In this section of his letter to the Church in Rome, the Apostle Paul points to the presence of the Holy Spirit as a sign of the saving power of Jesus at work.

Gospel: John 16:12-15
Today's Gospel reading comes from the Last Supper discourse in the Gospel of John. After having told the disciples that he must die in order for the Holy Spirit to come, Jesus explains that this Spirit will continue to reveal the things of God to them.

SOLEMNITY OF THE BODY AND BLOOD OF CHRIST

CYCLE A

First Reading: Deuteronomy 8:2-3, 14-16
Although the setting for today's first reading is Moses' final address to the people Israel before they entered the Promised Land, the text was actually written hundreds of years later when the people are anticipating a return to Judea following their exile in Babylon. This passage encourages the people to remember how God has always provided for them, even when the situation seemed most hopeless, and suggests that it is God's word which provides authentic life.

Second Reading: 1 Corinthians 10:16-17
The second reading's brief, but important, excerpt from a Pauline letter teaches that the Body of Christ refers not just to bread and wine, but to the unified communion of the people of God, the Church.

Gospel: John 6:51-58
Today's Gospel reading is part of the bread of life discourse in the Gospel of John. Possibly a sermon preached in John's church, the text declares that those who feed on Jesus, the Word of God, share in the transcendent life of God.

CYCLE B

First Reading: Exodus 24:3-8
All of today's Scripture readings are concerned with the idea of "covenant"—the bonding of a community of people to God.

   The first reading from the book of Exodus describes the ceremony at Mount Sinai that formally bonds God and the people of Israel for all eternity. In the Hebrew culture, blood was understood to be the liquid essence of life. By sprinkling blood upon the altar, which represents God, and then upon the people, Moses ritually links God and Israel in a perpetual sharing of life.

Second Reading: Hebrews 9:11-15
In the second reading, an unknown Christian writer reflects on how the death of Jesus echoes the Sinai covenant. Jesus' blood brings about an intensified and renewed bonding with the eternal life of God.

Gospel: Mark 14:12-16, 22-26
In the following excerpt from Mark's Last Supper account, Jesus speaks of his body and blood as a sacrifice that will bring about the reign of God. The covenant in the blood of Christ binds the Church and God together. Therefore, when we partake of the Lord's Supper today, our communion or bond with God in Christ is renewed.

CYCLE C

First Reading: Genesis 14:18-20
All of today's Scripture readings refer to God being made present through the ritual use of bread and wine.

   In the first reading from the book of Genesis, Abram encounters a mysterious figure named Melchizedek, whose name means "the king is just." The ruler of Salem, the future Jerusalem, this person is, remarkably, also a priest to the one true God. He thus anticipates the kingship and priesthood that will later dwell in Jerusalem. With bread and wine he invokes God's blessing on Abram.

Second Reading: Corinthians 11:23-26
Today's excerpt from Paul's letters is the oldest biblical account of the Last Supper. The Apostle understands that Christ's death is proclaimed whenever Christians share the bread and cup.

Gospel: Luke 9:11-17
The feeding of the multitude as presented by Luke might remind us of our Eucharists today. The bread that is blessed, broken, and shared among us nourishes our lives as Christ's followers in the present.

VIGIL OF THE ASSUMPTION
August 15

CYCLES A, B, C

First Reading: 1 Chronicles 15:3-4, 15-16; 16:1-2
The ark of the covenant in the Hebrew tradition marked the point of contact between God and the world. In this reading from the Hebrew Scriptures, David brings the ark into Jerusalem, thereby establishing his capital as the city in which God dwells.

Second Reading: 1 Corinthians 15:54-57
In this selection from a letter to the church in Corinth, the Apostle Paul praises God for conquering death by raising Christ to new life.

Gospel: Luke 11:27-28
The Gospel of Luke presents Mary, the mother of Jesus, as the first disciple of Jesus. Even though she could be praised for being the bearer, or ark, of the Son of God, the following passage indicates that she really should be praised for other reasons.

SOLEMNITY OF THE ASSUMPTION

CYCLES A, B, C

First Reading: Revelation 11:19; 12:1-6, 10
The book of Revelation was composed during a great persecution of
the Church by the Roman Emperor. It is written in a highly symbolic
style in order to protect the author and his readers from Roman as-
sault. In this excerpt, a woman who personifies the people of Israel
gives birth to a child who will defeat the Roman Empire and all
forces of evil. Christians often think of Mary, the mother of Jesus,
when reading this passage.

Second Reading: 1 Corinthians 15:20-26
In his letter to the Church in Corinth, the Apostle Paul assures his
Gentile converts that all who have died in Christ will be raised to a
glorious new existence just as Christ was.

Gospel: Luke 1:39-56
The infancy narrative in Luke's Gospel provides parallel accounts of
the births of Jesus and John the Baptizer. In this reading, their moth-
ers meet and the mother of Jesus praises the God who has blessed her
and who is acting to fulfill the ancient promises to Israel.

SOLEMNITY OF ALL SAINTS
November 1

CYCLES A, B, C

First Reading: Revelation 7:2-4, 9-14
The book of Revelation was written during a terrible persecution of
Christians by order of the Roman emperor at the end of the first century. In the following excerpt, the writer imagines the final victory of
the saints who have persevered in their faith despite the threat of
torture.

Second Reading: 1 John 3:1-3
In this passage from the First Letter of John, the author recognizes that believers are often rejected by the world. Nevertheless, they will ultimately share in Christ's glory.

Gospel: Matthew 5:1-12
The following portion of the Sermon on the Mount from Matthew's Gospel describes the attitudes that should characterize those who strive for holiness.

7. Recommended Resources

General Reference Works on the Bible

Brown, Raymond E., Joseph A. Fitzmyer, and Roland E. Murphy, eds. *The New Jerome Biblical Commentary.* Englewood Cliffs, N.J.: Prentice Hall, 1990.

Mays, James L., gen. ed. *Harper's Bible Commentary.* San Francisco: Harper and Row, 1988.

Church Documents on Jewish-Christian Relations or the Bible with Special Relevance for Lectionary Introductions

Bishops' Committee for Ecumenical and Interreligious Affairs, National Conference of Catholic Bishops. *Criteria for the Evaluation of Dramatizations of the Passion.* Washington: United States Catholic Conference, 1988.

Bishops' Committee on the Liturgy, National Conference of Catholic Bishops. *God's Mercy Endures Forever: Guidelines on the Presentation of Jews and Judaism in Catholic Preaching.* Washington: United States Catholic Conference, 1988.

Fisher, Eugene J., and Leon Klenicki, eds. *In Our Time: The Flowering of Jewish-Catholic Dialogue.* New York/Mahwah: Paulist Press/Stimulus Books, 1990.

Pontifical Biblical Commission. "Instruction on the Historical Truth of the Gospels," in *A Christological Catechism: New Testament Answers* by Joseph A. Fitzmyer. New York/Ramsey: Paulist Press, 1982 (131–142).

Secretariat for Catholic-Jewish Relations, Bishops' Committee on Ecumenical and Interreligious Affairs, National Conference of Catholic Bishops. *Guidelines for Catholic-Jewish Relations.* 1985 Revision. Washington: United States Catholic Conference, 1985.

Vatican Commission for Religious Relations with the Jews, "Notes on the Correct Way to Present Jews and Judaism in Preaching and Catechesis in the Roman Catholic Church." *Origins* 15/7 (July 4, 1985) 102–107.

Jewish-Christian Relations and the Scriptures

Beck, Norman A. *Mature Christianity: The Recognition and Repudiation of the Anti-Jewish Polemic of the New Testament.* Selinsgrove: Susquehana University Press, 1985.

Cunningham, Philip A. *Education for Shalom: Religion Textbooks and the Enhancement of the Catholic and Jewish Relationship.* Collegeville: The Liturgical Press, 1995.

Efroymson, David P., Eugene J. Fisher, and Leon Klenicki, eds. *Within Context: Essays on Jews and Judaism in the New Testament.* Collegeville: The Liturgical Press, 1993.

Fisher, Eugene J. *Seminary Education and Christian-Jewish Relations: A Curriculum and Resource Handbook.* Washington: National Catholic Education Association, 1983.

Johnson, Luke T., "The New Testament's Anti-Jewish Slander and the Conventions of Ancient Polemic." *Journal of Biblical Literature* 108/3 (Fall, 1989) 419–441.

Richardson, Peter, ed. *Anti-Judaism in Early Christianity Vol 1: Paul and the Gospels.* Waterloo, Ontario: Wilfrid Laurier University Press, 1986.

Saperstein, Marc. *Moments of Crisis in Jewish-Christian Relations.* Philadelphia: Trinity Press, 1989.

Pawlikowski, John T., and James A. Wilde. *When Catholics Speak About Jews.* Chicago: Liturgy Training Publications, 1987.

Williamson, Clark M., and Ronald J. Allen. *Interpreting Difficult Texts: Anti-Judaism and Christian Preaching.* Philadelphia: Trinity Press, 1989.

Scriptural Studies

The general reference works listed above will provide more than adequate exegetical information for the composition of lectionary introductions. The following are recommended for those who might wish further study of the

Scriptures that are most often employed in the lectionary. Popular treatments are followed by an asterisk.

Alter, Robert. *The Art of Biblical Narrative.* New York: Basic Books, 1981.

_____. *The Art of Biblical Poetry.* New York: Basic Books, 1985.

Anderson, Bernhard W. *Out of the Depths: The Psalms Speak for Us Today.* Philadelphia: Westminster, rev. ed., 1983.

Blenkinsopp, Joseph. *The Pentateuch: An Introduction to the First Five Books of the Bible.* New York: Doubleday, 1992.

Boadt, Lawrence. *Reading the Old Testament: An Introduction.* New York: Paulist, 1983.*

Brown, Raymond E. *An Adult Christ at Christmas.* Collegeville: The Liturgical Press, 1984.*

_____. *The Birth of the Messiah: A Commentary on the Infancy Narratives in Matthew and Luke.* Garden City, N.Y.: Image Books, 1977.

_____. *A Coming Christ in Advent.* Collegeville: The Liturgical Press, 1988.*

_____. *A Crucified Christ in Holy Week.* Collegeville: The Liturgical Press, 1986.*

_____. *The Death of the Messiah: From Gethsemane to the Grave, A Commentary on the Passion Narratives in the Four Gospels.* 2 vols. New York: Doubleday, 1994.

_____. *The Gospel According to John I–XII.* Anchor Bible 29. Garden City, N.Y.: Doubleday, 1966.

_____. *The Gospel According to John XIII–XXI.* Anchor Bible 29a. Garden City, N.Y.: Doubleday, 1970.

_____. *A Risen Christ in Eastertime.* Collegeville: The Liturgical Press, 1991.*

Brueggemann, Walter. *Genesis.* Interpretation Commentary. Atlanta: John Knox, 1982.

Castel, Francois. *The History of Israel and Judah in Old Testament Times.* New York: Paulist, 1985.*

Childs, Brevard. *The Book of Exodus: A Critical, Theological Commentary.* Old Testament Library. Philadelphia: Westminster, 1974.

Coote, Robert B., and Mary P. Coote. *Power, Politics, and the Making of the Bible: An Introduction.* Minneapolis: Fortress, 1990.

Coote, Robert B., and David Robert Ord. *The Bible's First History: From Eden to the Court of David with the Yahwist.* Philadelphia: Fortress, 1989.

Cunningham, Philip A. *Jesus and the Evangelists: The Ministry of Jesus in the Synoptic Gospels.* Lanham, Md.: University Press of America, 1993.*

_____. *Jewish Apostle to the Gentiles: Paul As He Saw Himself.* Mystic, Conn.: Twenty-Third, 1986.*

Durham, John I. *Exodus.* Word Biblical Commentary. Waco, Tex.: Word Books, 1987.

Fitzmyer, Joseph A. *The Gospel According to Luke I–IX.* Anchor Bible 28. Garden City, N.Y.: Doubleday, 1981.

_____. *The Gospel According to Luke X–XXIV.* Anchor Bible 28a. Garden City, N.Y.: Doubleday, 1983.

_____. *Paul and His Theology: A Brief Sketch.* Englewood Cliffs, N.J.: Prentice Hall, 1989.

Gottwald, Norman K. *The Hebrew Bible: A Socio-Literary Introduction.* Philadelphia: Fortress, 1985.

Hanson, Paul D. *The People Called: The Growth of Community in the Bible.* San Francisco: Harper & Row, 1986.

L'Heureux, Conrad E. *In and Out of Paradise: The Book of Genesis from Adam and Eve to the Tower of Babel.* New York: Paulist, 1983.*

Harrington, Daniel J. *The Gospel of Matthew.* Sacra Pagina 1. Collegeville: The Liturgical Press/Michael Glazier, 1991.

Heschel, Abraham. *The Prophets.* Vol. 11. New York: Harper & Row, 1975.*

Johnson, Luke Timothy. *The Gospel of Luke.* Sacra Pagina 3. Collegeville: The Liturgical Press/Michael Glazier, 1991.

King, Philip J. *Amos, Hosea, Micah—An Archaeological Commentary.* Philadelphia: Westminster, 1988.*

Klein, Ralph W. *Israel in Exile: A Theological Interpretation.* Philadelphia: Fortress, 1979.

Lachs, Samuel Tobias. *A Rabbinic Commentary on the New Testament: The Gospels of Matthew, Mark, and Luke*. Hoboken, N.J.: KTAV; New York: Anti-Defamation League of B'nai B'rith, 1987.

Mann, Thomas W. *The Book of the Torah: The Narrative Integrity of the Pentateuch*. Atlanta: John Knox, 1988.

McKenzie, John L. *Second Isaiah*. Anchor Bible 20. Garden City, N.Y.: Doubleday, 1968.

Murphy-O'Connor, Jerome. *Becoming Human Together: The Pastoral Anthropology of St. Paul*. Wilmington, Del.: Michael Glazier, 1982.

Neyrey, Jerome H. *An Ideology of Revolt: John's Christology in Social Science Perspective*. Philadelphia: Fortress Press, 1988.

Overman, J. Andrew. *Matthew's Gospel and Formative Judaism: The Social World of the Matthean Community*. Minneapolis: Fortress Press, 1991.

Perkins, Pheme. *Reading the New Testament: An Introduction*. 2d ed. New York: Paulist, 1988.*

Roetzel, Calvin. *The Letters of Paul: Conversations in Context*. 3d. ed. Atlanta: John Knox, 1991.

Saldarini, Anthony J. "Delegitimation of Leaders in Matthew 23." *Catholic Biblical Quarterly* 54/4 (October, 1992) 659–680.

_____. *Matthew's Christian-Jewish Community*. Chicago: University of Chicago Press, 1994.

_____. *Pharisees, Scribes, and Sadducees in Palestinian Society*. Wilmington, Del.: Michael Glazier, Inc., 1988.

Sarna, Nahum M. *Exploring Exodus*. New York: Schocken, 1986.*

_____. *Exodus*. JPS Torah Commentary. Philadelphia: Jewish Publications Society, 1991.

_____. *Genesis*. JPS Torah Commentary. Philadelphia: Jewish Publications Society, 1989.

_____. *Understanding Genesis*. New York: Schocken, 1966.*

Schnackenburg, Rudolph. *The Gospel According to St. John*. 3 vols. New York: Crossroad, 1982.

Skinner, John. *Genesis.* International Critical Commentary. Edinburgh: T & T Clark, 2d ed., 1930.

Speiser, E. A. *Genesis.* Anchor Bible 1. Garden City, N.Y.: Doubleday, 1964.

Terrien, Samuel. *The Elusive Presence: Toward a New Biblical Theology.* New York: Harper & Row, 1978.